Strategic Family Systems Intervention for AB-PA: Contingent Visitation Schedule

C.A. Childress, Psy.D.

Strategic Family Systems Intervention for AB-PA: Contingent Visitation Schedule

Oaksong Press, Claremont, California

Copyright © 2017 Craig Childress

Printed in the United States of America

ISBN 978-0-9961145-5-4

All Rights Reserved

Table of Contents

Case Conceptualization 1

Assessment and Diagnosis 11

Strategic Family Systems Intervention 19

Appendix 1: Research Studies on Parental Psychological Control
        of the Child Identified by Barber & Harmon 2002 29

Appendix 2: Treatment-Focused Assessment Protocol 35

Appendix 3: Sample Treatment-Focused Assessment Reports 39

Appendix 4: Diagnostic Checklist for Pathogenic Parenting 47

Appendix 5: Parenting Practices Rating Scale 51

Appendix 6: Parent-Child Relationship Rating Scale 55

1 Case Conceptualization

The case conceptualization in clinical psychology is the organizing framework for treatment and is based on the clinical diagnosis obtained from the assessment. The case conceptualization represents the overarching integration of assessment data into a diagnosis regarding the cause of the pathology, which then guides the development of the treatment plan to address and resolve the causal origins of the pathology. The foundational principle of clinical psychology is that assessment leads to diagnosis, and diagnosis guides treatment.

Organizing the symptom information into an overarching case conceptualization and diagnosis that then leads to the development of the treatment plan is accomplished through a three-step data collection and integration process (Schwitzer & Rubin, 2015):[1]

- Problem Identification: This phase involves the collection of relevant symptom and context data.
- Thematic Groupings: The clinical data is then organized into coherent themes.
- Theoretical Inferences: Established theoretical constructs and principles from professional psychology are then applied to the themes evidenced in the data to diagnose why the problems exist; this is the phase of developing the over-arching case conceptualization that will integrate assessment data with diagnosis, and diagnosis with treatment.

The development of the treatment plan is based on the clinical diagnosis, and the clinical diagnosis is embedded in the case conceptualization regarding the causal origins of the pathology. Assessment leads to diagnosis, and diagnosis guides treatment.

An inadequate assessment will lead to a flawed diagnosis and failed treatment. Developing an effective treatment plan begins with an appropriate assessment, which then leads to the development of the case conceptualization and clinical diagnosis regarding the causal origins of the pathology.

Differential Diagnosis of Attachment-Related Pathology

Assessing a child's rejection of a parent surrounding divorce requires an appropriate collection of relevant data regarding the child's symptoms. The clinical data is then organized into coherent themes, and standard and established constructs and principles of professional psychology are then applied to the clinical data to develop an organizing case conceptualization, diagnosis, and treatment plan. The collection of data during the assessment is guided by a process called "differential diagnosis," in which all of the alternative causal explanations for the

---

[1] Schwitzer, A.M. & Rubin, L.C. (2015). Diagnosis & treatment planning skills: A popular culture casebook approach (2nd ed.). Thousand Oak, CA: Sage.

symptoms are considered and data is systematically collected that will either confirm or disconfirm each of the differential diagnostic possibilities, ultimately leading to the final causal diagnosis.

A child's rejection of a parent is fundamentally an attachment-related pathology. The attachment system is the brain system that governs all aspects of love and bonding throughout the lifespan, including grief and loss. The attachment system is the brain system responsible for motivating parent-child bonding, and a child's rejection of a parent is fundamentally an attachment-related pathology.

The attachment system is a primary motivational system of the brain that developed across millions of years of evolution through the selective targeting of children by predators. Children who formed strong attachment bonds to parents were more likely to receive parental protection from predators, so that the genes of these children that motivated them to form strong attachment bonds to their parents would be selectively increased in the collective gene pool. On the other hand, children who bonded less strongly to their parents were more likely to fall prey to predation (and to other environmental dangers), so that the genes of these children that less-strongly motivated these children's attachment bonding to parents were selectively and systematically removed from the collective gene pool. Through the evolutionary pressures created by the selective predation of children, a very strong and highly resilient primary motivational system developed in the brain that powerfully motivates children to form strong and resilient attachment bonds to parents.

Children do not reject parents, not even problematic parents. A problematic parent more fully exposes children to predation and other environmental dangers. Children who rejected a problematic parent were far more likely to die from predation, environmental dangers, starvation, and neglect. The genes of children who rejected problematic parents were systematically and selectively removed from the collective gene pool over the evolutionary processes that created the attachment system. Conversely, children who responded to problematic parenting by becoming MORE strongly motivated to bond to the problematic parent were more likely to continue to receive parental protection and care. The genes of these children for promoting _increased_ child motivation to bond to a problematic parent would therefore become selected for by providing an increased survival advantage to the children of problematic parents, and the genes that MORE strongly motivated children to bond to problematic parents would increase in the collective gene. Problematic parenting creates an "insecure attachment" that MORE strongly motivates children to form an attachment bond to their parents.

A child rejecting a parent is an extremely unusual and aberrant display of the attachment bonding system that is entirely _inconsistent_ with the normal-range functioning of the child's attachment system. Since the attachment system is a neurologically embedded primary motivational system of the brain, it functions in characteristic ways and it dysfunctions in characteristic ways. Children do _not_ reject parents, not even problematic parents (and especially not problematic parents since rejecting a problematic parent would more fully expose the child to predation and other environmental dangers).

Since children's attachment bonding to parents confers such substantial survival advantage to children, the attachment system – a primary motivational system of the brain - _never_ spontaneously dysfunctions. The attachment system ONLY becomes dysfunctional in response to pathogenic parenting (patho=pathology; genic=genesis, creation). Pathogenic parenting is the creation of significant psychopathology in the child through highly aberrant and distorted parenting practices. The construct of pathogenic parenting is an established construct in both developmental and clinical psychology and is most often used in descriptions of attachment-related pathology since the attachment system only becomes dysfunctional in response to pathogenic parenting.

The attachment-related pathology of a child rejecting a parent is a clear symptom indicator of pathogenic parenting, either by the targeted-rejected parent (e.g., through chronic and severe parental abuse of the child), or by the allied and supposedly "favored" parent who has formed a _cross-generational coalition_ with the child against the other parent (Haley, 1977; Minuchin, 1974)[2] that is resulting in an *emotional cutoff* (Bowen, 1978; Titelman, 2003)[3] of the child's relationship with the targeted-rejected parent. The child's attachment-related pathology can ONLY be caused through pathogenic parenting by one parent or the other. It then becomes a process of differential diagnosis to determine which parent is creating the child's attachment-related pathology.

The Flawed Construct of "Parental Alienation"

A child rejecting a parent surrounding divorce has come to be called "parental alienation" in the popular culture, and the popularized construct of "parental alienation" has even been adopted by many mental health professionals. However, the construct of "parental alienation" is extremely problematic from a clinical psychology perspective for guiding professional assessment, diagnosis, and treatment.

In actuality, there is no adequately defined pathology in professional psychology for "parental alienation." The construct of "parental alienation" as a form of pathology originates in a proposal made in the mid-1980s by a psychiatrist, Richard Gardner, who proposed that a child's rejection of one parent surrounding divorce because of the negative parental influence applied to the child by the other parent supposedly reflected a new form of pathology in mental health – a "new syndrome" – which he called "Parental Alienation Syndrome" (PAS). Gardner's proposal for a new form of pathology that was supposedly unique in all of mental health was ill-conceived and was unfounded in the scientific and theoretical literature of professional psychology.

In proposing the existence of a new form of pathology – a "new syndrome" – Gardner bypassed the step of professional diagnosis and case conceptualization that involves the application of standard and established constructs and principles of professional psychology to a set of symptoms. Instead of following established professional practice of applying standard and established professional constructs and principles to the set of symptoms he observed, Gardner opted for what is a conceptually indolent and professionally inappropriate approach of simply proposing a new form of pathology that was supposedly unique in all of mental health, and that then required an equally unique new set of symptom identifiers created by Gardner specifically for this supposedly new form of pathology.

While Gardner was correct in identifying a form of pathology surrounding divorce in which the child is manipulated by one parent (the allied and supposedly "favored" parent) into rejecting a relationship with the other parent following divorce, Gardner was incorrect in proposing that this represented a new form of pathology – a "new syndrome" - that was unique in all of mental health. The pathology Gardner identified surrounding a child's rejection of a parent is <u>not</u> a new form of pathology. It is an attachment-related pathology called "pathological mourning" (Bowlby, 1980)[4] and a defined family systems pathology involving the child's *triangulation* into the spousal conflict through the formation of a *cross-generational coalition* with an allied parent against the targeted parent that creates an *emotional cutoff* in the child's relationship with the targeted parent (Bowen, 1975; Haley, 1977; Minuchin 1974). Gardner simply skipped the step of professional diagnosis by proposing that the symptoms he observed represented a new form of pathology unique in all of mental health – a "new syndrome" – rather that applying the professional rigor necessary to diagnose the pathology from within the

---

[2] Haley, J. (1977). Toward a theory of pathological systems. In P. Watzlawick & J. Weakland (Eds.), The interactional view (pp. 31-48). New York: Norton.

Minuchin, S. (1974). Families and family therapy. Harvard University Press.

[3] Bowen, M. (1978). Family Therapy in Clinical Practice. New York: Jason Aronson.

Titelman, P. (2003). Emotional cutoff in Bowen family systems theory: An Overview. In Emotional cutoff: Bowen family systems theory perspectives, P. Titelman (ed). New York: Haworth Press.

[4] Bowlby, J. (1980). Attachment and loss: Vol. 3. Loss: Sadness and depression. NY: Basic Books.

standard and established constructs and principles of professional psychology. Gardner was simply a poor diagnostician.

In skipping the step of professional diagnosis, Gardner led professional psychology off of the path of established professional practice and into the wilderness of a supposedly "new form of pathology" that was ill conceived and poorly defined, and that lacked established scientific support and theoretical foundation. In leading professional psychology into the wilderness of supposedly new forms of pathology, Gardner's construct of "parental alienation" created a schism in professional psychology between ardent adherents and equally ardent detractors for Gardner's proposal of a new form of pathology. The proponents accurately noted the existence of the pathology, although in also failing to appropriately diagnose the pathology using standard and established constructs and principles from professional psychology these adherents continued Gardner's fundamental diagnostic error. Meanwhile, the critics of Gardner's "parental alienation" pathology proposal accurately noted the absence of scientific support for a "new form of pathology" that was supposedly unique in all of mental health, along with accurate critiques of Gardner's ill-conceived symptom identifiers and his problematic case conceptualization surrounding this supposedly unique new form of pathology.

It is long-past overdue to correct Gardner's initial diagnostic error by returning to the established path of professional psychology and professional diagnosis. Diagnosis is the application of standard and established constructs and principles to a set of symptoms. Skipping the crucial step of professional diagnosis is the fundamental error made by Gardner in proposing a new form of pathology – a "new syndrome" – that was supposedly unique in all of mental health, and correcting this error and returning professional psychology to the path of established professional practice is the aim of an attachment-based model of "parental alienation" (AB-PA) that defines the attachment-related pathology of a child rejecting a parent surrounding divorce from entirely within the standard and established constructs and principles of professional psychology (Childress, 2015)[5]

An Attachment-Based Model of "Parental Alienation"

A child rejecting a parent is fundamentally an attachment-related pathology. John Bowlby, who first described the attachment system in his three volumes on bonding, separation, and loss (Bowlby, 1969, 1973, 1980)[6] indicated that the suppression of attachment bonding motivations is the product of "pathological mourning."

> "The deactivation of attachment behavior is a key feature of certain common variants of pathological mourning." (Bowlby, 1980, p. 70)

Bowlby further links pathological mourning to personality pathology that develops from adverse childhood experiences.

> "Disturbances of personality, which include a bias to respond to loss with disordered mourning, are seen as the outcome of one or more deviations in development that can originate or grow worse during any of the years of infancy, childhood and adolescence." (Bowlby, 1980, p. 217)

No sooner do we return to the established constructs and principles of professional psychology than we immediately identify the pathology as the pathological processing of sadness surrounding the divorce, and that this "disordered mourning" is related to personality pathology. Turning then to the field of personality disorder

---

[5] Childress, C.A. (2015). An attachment-based model of parental alienation: Foundations. Claremont, CA: Oaksong Press.

[6] Bowlby, J. (1969). Attachment and loss. Vol. 1. Attachment. NY: Basic Books.

[6] Bowlby, J. (1973). Attachment and loss: Vol. 2. Separation: Anxiety and anger. NY: Basic Books.

[6] Bowlby, J. (1980). Attachment and loss: Vol. 3. Loss: Sadness and depression. NY: Basic Books.

pathology, the preeminent expert in narcissistic and borderline personality pathology, Otto Kernberg, identifies that the narcissistic personality is characterologically unable to process sadness and "mournful longing," and instead translates feelings of sadness into anger and a desire for revenge;

> "They [narcissists] are especially deficient in genuine feelings of sadness and mournful longing; their incapacity for experiencing depressive reactions is a basic feature of their personalities. When abandoned or disappointed by other people they may show what on the surface looks like depression, but which on further examination emerges as anger and resentment, loaded with revengeful wishes, rather than real sadness for the loss of a person whom they appreciated." (Kernberg, 1977, p. 229)[7]

The pathology called "parental alienation" in the popular culture represents the attachment-related pathology of pathological mourning by a narcissistic/(borderline) personality parent who is translating feelings of sadness, grief, and loss surrounding the divorce into "anger and resentment, loaded with revengeful wishes" directed toward the ex-spouse (who has created a "narcissistic injury" by rejecting and abandoning the psychologically fragile narcissistic/(borderline) parent). In order for this narcissistic parent to then stabilize this parent's own collapsing personality pathology that is decompensating in response to the rejection and abandonment of the divorce, the narcissistic/(borderline) spouse-and-parent forms a **cross-generational coalition** with the child (Haley, 1977; Minuchin, 1974)[8] and manipulatively influences the child (Barber, 2002)[9] into rejecting the other parent/(spouse) by adopting a similar interpretation of the child's own feelings of sadness, grief, and loss surrounding the divorce as being "anger and resentment, loaded with revengeful wishes" directed toward the targeted parent.

Family Systems Pathology

Families must navigate a variety of transitions over their developmental course, beginning with the formation of a stable marriage, then integrating new roles as father and mother with the birth of the first child into their existing spousal roles of husband and wife. The family must then navigate transitions created during the different developmental phases of children's maturation that require differing parental responses, ultimately leading to the child's entry into adolescence and emerging independence, and the launching of children into young adulthood, leading to an "empty nest" within the spousal relationship. Divorce and the dissolution of the marital relationship represents one of the most impactful transitions any family must navigate; the transition from an intact family structure that was previously united by the marriage, to a new separated family structure that is now united by the children through the continuing co-parenting roles with the children, and by the continuing bonds of shared affections between the children and both parents.

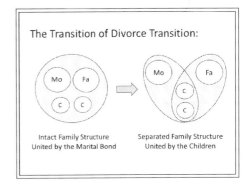

When pathology within the family prevents the successful transition to a new structural organization, symptoms develop within the family, often with the children, in order to stabilize the family's relationships (the family's "homeostatic balance") that are threatened with collapse in response to the family's unsuccessful adaptation to the demands of the family's new

---

[7] Kernberg, O.F. (1975). Borderline conditions and pathological narcissism. New York: Aronson.

[8] Haley, J. (1977). Toward a theory of pathological systems. In P. Watzlawick & J. Weakland (Eds.), The interactional view (pp. 31-48). New York: Norton.

Minuchin, S. (1974). Families and family therapy. Harvard University Press.

[9] Barber, B. K. (Ed.) (2002). Intrusive parenting: How psychological control affects children and adolescents. Washington, DC: American Psychological Association.

organizational structure. One of the most common forms of family symptom is the "triangulation" of the child into the spousal conflict through the formation of a "cross-generational coalition" with one parent (the allied parent) against the other parent (the targeted parent). The cross-generational coalition of the parent with the child is used by the allied parent to divert the **spousal** divorce-related anger of the allied parent toward the other **spouse** through the child's continuing relationship with the targeted parent. The child essentially becomes a proxy weapon used by the allied parent in this parent's spousal conflict with the other spouse-parent.

The preeminent family systems therapist, Jay Haley, provides the following definition for the cross-generational coalition:

> "The people responding to each other in the triangle are not peers, but one of them is of a different generation from the other two... In the process of their interaction together, the person of one generation forms a coalition with the person of the other generation against his peer. By 'coalition' is meant a process of joint action which is *against* the third person... The coalition between the two persons is denied. That is, there is certain behavior which indicates a coalition which, when it is queried, will be denied as a coalition... In essence, the perverse triangle is one in which the separation of generations is breached in a covert way. When this occurs as a repetitive pattern, the system will be pathological." (Haley, 1977, p. 37)[10]

One of the characteristic features of a cross-generational coalition within the family is an "inverted family hierarchy," in which the child becomes elevated in the family hierarchy through the empowerment and support the child receives from the coalition with the allied and supposedly "favored" parent. In an inverted family hierarchy, the child occupies an elevated position <u>above</u> the targeted parent, from which the child then feels empowered and entitled to judge the adequacy of the targeted parent as both a parent and a person. Meanwhile, the allied and supposedly "favored" parent who has formed the cross-generational coalition with the child against the other parent, actively, yet covertly, supports the child's hostility toward the other parent/(spouse) by offering parental displays of comfort and "understanding" to the child surrounding the child's conflict with the other parent/(spouse).

On page 42 of their book *Family Healing: Strategies for Hope and Understanding* (Minuchin & Nichols, 1993),[11] the preeminent family systems therapist Salvador Minuchin and his co-author Michael Nichols provide a structural family diagram for a **cross-generational coalition** of a father and child, and the ensuing **emotional cutoff** (Bowen, 1978; Titelman, 2003)[12] in the relationship with the mother that is created by this cross-generational coalition in the family. Note the triangular pattern to the family's relationships as the child is drawn into the spousal conflict by the cross-generational coalition with the father against the mother, thereby turning the two-person marital conflict into a three-person spouse-child-spouse triangulated conflict. The covert support the child receives from the cross-generational coalition with the allied parent empowers the child into an elevated position in the family hierarchy above that of the mother (an "inverted family hierarchy") from which the child feels entitled to judge the adequacy of the mother as a parent and as a person, supported by the empowering coalition with the father.

Structural diagram of triangulation, cross-generational coalition, inverted hierarchy, enmeshment, and cutoff.
(Minuchin & Nichols, 1993, p. 42)

---

[10] Haley, J. (1977). Toward a theory of pathological systems. In P. Watzlawick & J. Weakland (Eds.), The interactional view (pp. 31-48). New York: Norton.

[11] Minuchin. S. & Nichols, M.P. (1993). Family healing: Strategies for hope and understanding. New York: Touchstone.

[12] Bowen, M. (1978). Family Therapy in Clinical Practice. New York: Jason Aronson.

Titelman, P. (2003). Emotional cutoff in Bowen family systems theory: An Overview. In Emotional cutoff: Bowen family systems theory perspectives, P. Titelman (ed). New York: Haworth Press.

The three lines between the father and child in this diagram indicate a psychologically "enmeshed" relationship reflecting a boundary violation by the father of the child's independent psychological autonomy.

In his seminal book on family therapy, *Families and Family Therapy* (1974),[13] Salvador Minuchin provides a clinical case example for the impact of a cross-generational coalition on family relationships surrounding divorce:

> "An inappropriately rigid cross-generational subsystem of mother and son versus father appears, and the boundary around this coalition of mother and son excludes the father. A cross-generational dysfunctional transactional pattern has developed" (p. 61-62)

> "The parents were divorced six months earlier and the father is now living alone… Two of the children who were very attached to their father, now refuse any contact with him. The younger children visit their father but express great unhappiness with the situation." (p. 101)

This clinical description by Minuchin of the children "refusing any contact" with their father following the parents' divorce because of the "cross-generational subsystem of the mother and son versus the father," in which the "coalition of mother and son excludes the father," exactly captures the pathology commonly called "parental alienation" in the common culture.

In his definition of the cross-generational coalition, Haley (1977)[14] refers to the cross-generational coalition as a "perverse triangle" because the allied parent's coalition with the child represents a **boundary violation** of the child's psychological integrity through the parent's psychological manipulation, seduction, and coercive control of the child in order to meet the emotional and psychological needs of the allied parent. In the *Journal of Emotional Abuse*, Kerig (2005)[15] identifies four types of psychological boundary violations in the parent-child relationship, and links the dissolution of psychological boundaries in the parent-child relationship to the subsequent emotional abuse of the child;

> "Examination of the theoretical and empirical literatures suggests that there are four distinguishable dimensions to the phenomenon of boundary dissolution: role reversal, intrusiveness, enmeshment, and spousification." (Kerig, 2005, p. 8)

> "The breakdown of appropriate generational boundaries between parents and children significantly increases the risk for emotional abuse… In the throes of their own insecurity, troubled parents may rely on the child to meet the parent's emotional needs, turning to the child to provide the parent with support, nurturance, or comforting. Ultimately, preoccupation with the parents' needs threatens to interfere with the child's ability to develop autonomy, initiative, self-reliance, and a secure internal working model of the self and others." (Kerig, 2005, p. 6)

Superficially, the cross-generational coalition of the child with the allied parent may appear to be an emotionally bonded parent-child relationship. However, it is <u>not</u> a psychologically healthy parent-child bond. Instead, the parentally manipulative, intrusive, and hyper-bonded relationship between the allied parent and child who have formed a cross-generational coalition is being used by the allied parent to meet this parent's own emotional insecurities and psychological needs. By psychologically seducing and manipulating the child into becoming a weapon to be used against the other spouse-parent, the allied parent is using the child in a highly

---

[13] Minuchin, S. (1974). Families and family therapy. Harvard University Press.

[14] Haley, J. (1977). Toward a theory of pathological systems. In P. Watzlawick & J. Weakland (Eds.), The interactional view (pp. 31-48). New York: Norton.

[15] Kerig, P.K. (2005). Revisiting the construct of boundary dissolution: A multidimensional perspective. Journal of Emotional Abuse, 5, 5-42.

pathological *role-reversal relationship* to meet the emotional and psychological needs of the allied narcissistic/(borderline) personality parent.

Through pathogenic parenting practices of psychological control and manipulation, the allied narcissistic/(borderline) personality parent creates a cross-generational alliance with the child against the normal-range and affectionally available targeted parent. The function served by the cross-generational coalition is to divert the allied parent's **spousal** anger toward the other **spouse** through the child by using the child's relationship with the other parent as a means to inflict emotional suffering on the other parent through the parent-child conflict, and when the allied parent has borderline personality pathology, to also allay the borderline parent's abandonment fears that were triggered by the divorce. Through the cross-generational coalition, the child is induced into expressing hostility toward and/or a complete rejection of the other parent for alleged parental inadequacies and failures that have their origin the spousal inadequacy beliefs of the allied parent, and that become co-manufactured as supposed parental inadequacies in the cross-generational coalition with the allied parent.

Psychological Control: Creating the Child's Pathology

The allied parent creates the child's rejection of the other parent through covert techniques of psychological control and manipulation in which a "loyalty bind" is created for the child of being forced to choose sides in the spousal conflict. The allied narcissistic/(borderline) parent then manipulatively distorts the child's normal-range sadness surrounding the divorce into blame of the other parent, and into the same "anger and resentment, loaded with revengeful wishes" experienced by the allied narcissistic/(borderline) parent directed at the other parent for supposedly causing the breakup of the family. Through manipulative communication exchanges with the child, the allied parent ultimately leads the child into a false belief that the child is being "victimized" by the normal-range parenting of the other parent. Once the child adopts the "victimized child" role, this then allows the allied parent to adopt and conspicuously display to others the coveted role as the supposedly "protective parent," while the targeted parent is falsely cast into the role as a supposedly bad and "abusive parent."

All of this is a false narrative – a false story – created by the manipulative parenting practices of the allied parent who manipulates the child into adopting a role of the "victimized child" relative to the other parent. This false drama represents a reenactment of a storyline from the allied parent's own childhood attachment trauma (that led to the formation of this parent's narcissistic and/or borderline personality pathology). The pathology traditionally called "parental alienation" in the popular culture represents a complex attachment-related pathology of a pathological processing of sadness surrounding the divorce, and the trans-generational transmission of childhood attachment-related trauma from the childhood of a narcissistic and/or borderline personality parent to the current family relationships, mediated by the narcissistic and borderline personality pathology of the allied parent, which is itself a product of this parent's childhood attachment trauma (Childress, 2015).[16]

Parental psychological control and manipulation of the child's thoughts and feelings is an established construct in professional psychology. In his book, *Intrusive Parenting: How Psychological Control Affects Children and Adolescents* (2002),[17] published by the American Psychological Association, Brian Barber and his colleague,

---

[16] Childress, C.A. (2015). An attachment-based model of parental alienation: Foundations. Claremont, CA: Oaksong Press.

[17] Barber, B. K. (Ed.) (2002). Intrusive parenting: How psychological control affects children and adolescents. Washington, DC: American Psychological Association.

Elizabeth Harmon (Barber & Harmon, 2002),[18] cite over 30 empirically validated scientific studies measuring the construct of parental psychological control with children, and nearly 20 additional studies on constructs related to psychological control (Appendix 1). Barber and Harmon provide the following definition of parental psychological control of the child:

> "Psychological control refers to parental behaviors that are intrusive and manipulative of children's thoughts, feelings, and attachment to parents. These behaviors appear to be associated with disturbances in the psychoemotional boundaries between the child and parent, and hence with the development of an independent sense of self and identity." (Barber & Harmon, 2002, p. 15)

Stone, Buehler, and Barber (2002)[19] describe the process of the psychological control of children by parents:

> "Parental psychological control is defined as verbal and nonverbal behaviors that intrude on youth's emotional and psychological autonomy... The central elements of psychological control are intrusion into the child's psychological world and self-definition and parental attempts to manipulate the child's thoughts and feelings through invoking guilt, shame, and anxiety. Psychological control is distinguished from behavioral control in that the parent attempts to control, through the use of criticism, dominance, and anxiety or guilt induction, the youth's thoughts and feelings rather than the youth's behavior." (Stone, Buehler, and Barber, 2002, p. 57)

Soenens and Vansteenkiste (2010)[20] describe the various methods used to achieve parental psychological control of the child:

> "Psychological control can be expressed through a variety of parental tactics, including (a) guilt-induction, which refers to the use of guilt inducing strategies to pressure children to comply with a parental request; (b) contingent love or love withdrawal, where parents make their attention, interest, care, and love contingent upon the children's attainment of parental standards; (c) instilling anxiety, which refers to the induction of anxiety to make children comply with parental requests; and (d) invalidation of the child's perspective, which pertains to parental constraining of the child's spontaneous expression of thoughts and feelings." (Soenens & Vansteenkiste, 2010, p. 75)

Research by Stone, Buehler, and Barber establishes the link between parental psychological control of children and marital conflict:

> "This study was conducted using two different samples of youth. The first sample consisted of youth living in Knox County, Tennessee. The second sample consisted of youth living in Ogden, Utah." (Stone, Buehler, and Barber, 2002, p. 62)

> "The analyses reveal that variability in psychological control used by parents is not random but it is linked to interparental conflict, particularly covert conflict. Higher levels of covert conflict in the marital relationship heighten the likelihood that parents would use psychological control with their children." (Stone, Buehler, and Barber, 2002, p. 86)

---

[18] Barber, B. K. and Harmon, E. L. (2002). Violating the self: Parenting psychological control of children and adolescents. In B. K. Barber (Ed.), Intrusive parenting (pp. 15-52). Washington, DC: American Psychological Association.

[19] Stone, G., Buehler, C., & Barber, B. K. (2002) Interparental conflict, parental psychological control, and youth problem behaviors. In B. K. Barber (Ed.), Intrusive parenting: How psychological control affects children and adolescents. Washington, DC.: American Psychological Association.

[20] Soenens, B., & Vansteenkiste, M. (2010). A theoretical upgrade of the concept of parental psychological control: Proposing new insights on the basis of self-determination theory. Developmental Review, 30, 74–99.

Stone, Buehler, and Barber provide an explanation for their finding that intrusive parental psychological control of children is related to high inter-spousal conflict:

> "The concept of triangles "describes the way any three people relate to each other and involve others in emotional issues between them" (Bowen, 1989, p. 306). In the anxiety-filled environment of conflict, a third person is triangulated, either temporarily or permanently, to ease the anxious feelings of the conflicting partners. By default, that third person is exposed to an anxiety-provoking and disturbing atmosphere. For example, a child might become the scapegoat or focus of attention, thereby transferring the tension from the marital dyad to the parent-child dyad. Unresolved tension in the marital relationship might spill over to the parent-child relationship through parents' use of psychological control as a way of securing and maintaining a strong emotional alliance and level of support from the child. As a consequence, the triangulated youth might feel pressured or obliged to listen to or agree with one parents' complaints against the other. The resulting enmeshment and cross-generational coalition would exemplify parents' use of psychological control to coerce and maintain a parent-youth emotional alliance against the other parent (Haley, 1976; Minuchin, 1974)." (Stone, Buehler, and Barber, 2002, p. 86-87)

Barber and Harmon reference the established research regarding the damage that this violation of the child's psychological integrity has on the child:

> "Numerous elements of the child's self-in-relation-to-parent have been discussed as being compromised by psychologically controlling behaviors such as **individuality** (Goldin, 1969; Kurdek, et al., 1995; Litovsky & Dusek, 1985; Schaefer, 1965a, 1965b, Steinberg, Lamborn, Dornbusch, & Darling, 1992); **individuation** (Barber et al., 1994; Barber & Shagle, 1992; Costanzo & Woody, 1985; Goldin, 1969, Smetana, 1995; Steinberg & Silverberg, 1986; Wakschlag, Chase-Landsdale & Brooks-Gunn, 1996 1996); **independence** (Grotevant & Cooper, 1986; Hein & Lewko, 1994; Steinberg et al., 1994); **degree of psychological distance** between parents and children (Barber et al., 1994); and **threatened attachment** to parents (Barber, 1996; Becker, 1964)." (Barber & Harmon, 2002, p. 25; emphasis added).

Using the child as a weapon against the other spouse in the inter-spousal conflict surrounding divorce represents extremely bad parenting, and causing the child to lose a loving and bonded relationship with the other parent in order to meet the allied narcissistic/(borderline) parent's own needs for revenge and emotional stability is extraordinarily damaging to the child's healthy emotional and psychological development. Pathogenic parenting that creates significant psychopathology in the child in order to meet the emotional and psychological needs of the parent may rise to the level of a DSM-5 diagnosis of V995.51 Child Psychological Abuse.

Assessment leads to diagnosis, and diagnosis guides treatment. In all cases of attachment-related pathology surrounding divorce, it is vital that a proper assessment for possible pathogenic parenting by an allied narcissistic/(borderline) parent who is using the child as a weapon against the other spouse be conducted by a mental health professional who is knowledgeable and expert in the attachment system, personality disorder pathology as it affects family relationships, family systems therapy, and complex trauma as it is transmitted across generations.

2 Assessment & Diagnosis

Professional Competence

The pathology of attachment-based "parental alienation" (AB-PA; Childress, 2015)[21] represents the complex expression within the family of attachment-related pathology, parental narcissistic and/or borderline personality disorder pathology, and family systems pathology, that originates from the trans-generational transmission of complex trauma. The complexity of the family pathology and the specialized professional expertise required for assessment and diagnosis qualifies the children and families evidencing the complex family pathology of AB-PA as a *special population* who require specialized professional knowledge and expertise to competently assess, diagnose and treat.

Mental health professionals who are assessing, diagnosing, and treating attachment-related pathology need to be professionally knowledgeable and competent in the attachment system, what it is, how it functions, and how it characteristically dysfunctions. Failure to possess the professional-level knowledge regarding the attachment system needed when assessing, diagnosing, and treating attachment-related pathology surrounding divorce would likely represent practice beyond the boundaries of professional competence in violation of professional standards of practice.

Mental health professionals who are assessing, diagnosing, and treating personality disorder pathology as it is affecting family relationships need to be professionally knowledgeable and competent in personality disorder pathology, what it is, how it functions, and how it characteristically affects family relationships following divorce. Failure to possess the necessary professional-level knowledge regarding personality disorder pathology when assessing, diagnosing, and treating personality disorder pathology in the family would likely represent practice beyond the boundaries of professional competence in violation of professional standards of practice.

Mental health professionals who are assessing, diagnosing, and treating families need to be professionally knowledgeable and competent in the functioning of family systems and the principles of family systems therapy. Failure to possess the necessary professional-level knowledge regarding the functioning of family systems and the principles of family systems therapy when assessing, diagnosing, and treating family pathology would likely represent practice beyond the boundaries of professional competence in violation of professional standards of practice.

Mental health professionals who are assessing, diagnosing, and treating the trans-generational transmission of complex trauma need to be professionally knowledgeable and competent in the nature of complex trauma, as expressed both individually and through family relationships. Failure to possess the required

---

[21] Childress, C.A. (2015). An attachment-based model of parental alienation: Foundations. Claremont, CA; Oaksong Press.

professional-level knowledge regarding the trans-generational transmission and expression of complex trauma needed when assessing, diagnosing, and treating family pathology involving complex trauma would likely represent practice beyond the boundaries of professional competence in violation of professional standards of practice.

Diagnostic Indicators

Resolving pathology begins with conducing a proper assessment, which then leads to formulating a case conceptualization and diagnosis regarding the cause of the pathology, which then leads, in turn, to the development of the treatment plan based on the case conceptualization and diagnosis. Assessment leads to diagnosis, and diagnosis guides treatment.

The attachment-related family pathology of an attachment-based model of "parental alienation" (AB-PA) as described in *Foundations* (Childress, 2015), can be consistently and reliably identified by the presence of three characteristic diagnostic indicators in the child's symptom display:

1. **Attachment System Suppression:** The suppression of the child's attachment bonding motivations toward a normal-range and affectionally available parent. The attachment system never spontaneously dysfunctions, but ONLY becomes dysfunctional in response to pathogenic parenting. The presence of diagnostic indicator 1 in the child's symptom display identifies the attachment origins of the pathology and indicates the presence of pathogenic parenting, either from the targeted-rejected parent (such as from severe and chronic child abuse), or from the allied parent through the formation of a cross-generational coalition with the child against the other parent.

2. **Personality Disorder Traits or Phobic Anxiety:** The presence in the child's symptom display of five specific a-priori predicted narcissistic personality traits:

    Grandiosity: The child is elevated into a grandiose position above the targeted-rejected parent from which the child sits in judgement of the targeted parent's adequacy as a parent and as a person.

    Entitlement: The child believes that they are entitled to have their every desire satisfied by the targeted-rejected parent to the child's satisfaction, or else the child feels entitled to exact a retaliatory punishment on the parent for allegedly inadequate parenting.

    Absence of Empathy: The child displays an absence of empathy for the emotional pain and suffering of the targeted-rejected parent caused by the child. The child asserts the theme that the targeted-rejected parent "deserves" to be rejected because of this parent's supposed inadequacy as a parent and as a person.

    Haughty Arrogance: The child displays an attitude of haughty and arrogant contempt and derision toward the targeted-rejected parent for this parent's supposed inadequacy as a parent and as a person.

    Splitting: The child displays a polarized perception of idealization for the allied parent and demonization of the targeted-rejected parent, and the child is unable to envision and accept changes to the child's fixed beliefs surrounding the targeted-rejected parent.

    Phobic Anxiety Variant: The child might also report and display an excessively elevated anxiety surrounding the targeted-rejected parent, either instead of the narcissistic personality traits or in addition to the narcissistic personality traits. When present, this symptom of excessively elevated anxiety will meet DSM-5 diagnostic criteria for a Specific Phobia, but of a bizarre and unrealistic "mother type" or "father type" of phobia (no such pathology exists as a "mother phobia" or "father phobia").

> Persistent Unwarranted Fear: The child displays a persistent and unwarranted fear of the targeted-rejected parent that is cued either by the presence of the targeted parent or in anticipation of being in the presence of the targeted parent.
>
> Severe Anxiety Response: The presence of the targeted-rejected parent almost invariably provokes an anxiety response which can reach the levels of a situationally provoked panic attack.
>
> Avoidance of Parent: The child seeks to avoid exposure to the targeted parent due to the situationally provoked anxiety or else endures the presence of the targeted parent with great distress.

The presence in the child's symptom display of narcissistic personality traits and/or phobic anxiety toward a parent represent the "psychological fingerprint" evidence of the psychological control of the child by a narcissistic and/or borderline parent who is the source origin for these beliefs being expressed by the child.

3. **Encapsulated Persecutory Delusion:** The child evidences a fixed and false belief that is maintained despite contrary evidence (a delusion) regarding the child's supposed "victimization" by the normal-range parenting of the targeted-rejected parent (an encapsulated persecutory delusion). The presence in the child's symptom display of an encapsulated persecutory delusion represents the symptom evidence of the child's adoption of the "victimized child" role in the allied parent's false trauma reenactment narrative.

The presence in the child's symptom display of <u>all three</u> of these symptoms together represents definitive diagnostic evidence for the pathology of attachment-based "parental alienation" as defined in *Foundations* (Childress, 2015).[22] No other pathological process in all of mental health will produce all three of these symptom features in the child's symptom display other than the pathology of attachment-based parental alienation (AB-PA) as described in *Foundations*.

Associated Clinical Signs

Diagnosis, however, is more than simply identifying a limited set of symptoms. Diagnosis is putting together the entire pattern of symptoms and processes that represent the pathology. The entire pattern of symptoms leads to the case conceptualization, which provides the conceptual framework for organizing the pattern of symptoms into a collective meaning.

In addition to the three diagnostic indicators for an attachment-based model of "parental alienation" that represent the diagnostic evidence for the pathology of AB-PA, there are 12 *Associated Clinical Signs* that often co-occur in the pathology. While these 12 *Associated Clinical Signs* may or may not be present in any individual case, when present they represent strongly confirming additional diagnostic evidence for the pathology of AB-PA.

> **ACS-1: Use of the Word "Forced."** The allied parent or child uses the term "forced" in describing the child's opportunity to spend time with the targeted-rejected parent.
>
> **ACS-2: Empowering the Child to Reject the Parent.** The allied parent seeks to empower the child's rejection of the other parent.
>
>> Allied Parent: "The child should be allowed to decide on visitation."
>>
>> Allied Parent: "We need to listen to what the child wants."
>
> The allied parent seeks to have the child testify in court to reject the other parent.

---

[22] Childress, C.A. (2015). An attachment-based model of parental alienation: Foundations. Claremont, CA: Oaksong Press.

ACS-3: The Exclusion Demand. The child seeks to exclude the targeted-rejected parent from the child's activities, such as sporting events, awards ceremonies, musical concerts and recitals, school plays, etc.

ACS 4: Parental Replacement. The child begins to call the targeted-rejected parent by this parent's first name rather than by the possessive parental titles of "mom" or "dad," and/or the child begins to call the step-parent spouse of the allied parent by the parental titles of "mom" or "dad."

ACS-5: The Unforgivable Event: The child maintains that the reason for the child's rejection of the targeted parent is due to some past event that is supposedly too heinous to be forgiven.

ACS-6: "Liar" - "Fake." The child discounts the targeted parent's overtures of affection as the targeted parent being a "liar," and the child discounts and the targeted parent's signs of hurt at the child's rejection by alleging that the parental expression of hurt is "fake."

ACS-7: Themes for Rejection. The child's expresses one or more of the following characteristic themes for justifying the child's rejection of the targeted parent:

Too Controlling: That the targeted parent is too controlling and doesn't listen to what the child wants (including that the targeted parent doesn't acquiesce to child's desire to reject the targeted parent).

Anger Management: That the targeted parent is too prone to anger and anger dyscontrol (potentially provoked by the child's defiance and haughty arrogant attitude of contempt for the targeted parent).

Responsibility-Apology: That the targeted parent doesn't take responsibility and doesn't apologize for past failures in parenting (which the targeted parent disputes as actually having occurred or which represent entirely normal-range parenting in the context in which they occurred).

New Romantic Relationship: That the targeted parent's new romantic relationship or newly remarried spouse results in the targeted parent neglecting the child, leading the child to then reject the targeted parent (yet despite the child's supposed feelings of being neglected in time and attention, the child refuses opportunities to spend more time and receive more attention from the targeted parent).

Prior Non-Attention: That the targeted parent didn't spend adequate time with the child before the divorce so the child doesn't want to spend time with this parent now.

Vague Personhood of the Targeted Parent: The child asserts that the reason for rejection is something vague about the general personhood of the targeted parent.

Non-Forgivable Grudge: The child maintains that the reason for the current rejection is a past event that is supposedly so heinous that it cannot be forgiven.

Not Feeding the Child: The child (and the allied parent) assert that the targeted parent does not adequately feed the child.

ACS-8: Unwarranted Use of the Word "Abuse." The use of the term "abuse" entails two differential diagnostic possibilities, 1) authentic abuse, and 2) borderline personality traits in the person making the allegation. The term "abuse" is socially inflammatory and immediately provokes a risk management protective response from others. Normal-range people tend to use less inflammatory words, such as "mean," "cruel," "unkind," "rude," etc., and normal-range people tend to reserve the term "abuse" for more extreme situations of actual abuse. Borderline personalities, however, use the term "abuse" abundantly, partly because their "victimization" pathology perceives all interpersonal conflict as being "abusive," and partly to achieve a manipulative goal of obtaining a protective response from others who are recruited into being allies through the borderline personality presentation of victimization. All allegations of abuse should be fully and appropriately assessed. However, when the use of the term "abuse" is not warranted by the actual circumstances, then a differential diagnostic potential of possible borderline personality processes should receive additional assessment.

ACS-9: Excessive Texting & Phone Calls: The allied parent and child engage in excessive texting and phone contact during the child's time with the targeted parent that significantly disrupts the ability of the targeted parent to form a bonded relationship with the child.

ACS-10: Role-Reversal Use of the Child. The child is manipulatively placed out front as supposedly making an "independent" decision that just happens to coincidentally align with the desires of the allied parent, and that are opposed to the desires of the targeted parent. The allied parent then exploits the child's supposedly "independent" decisions to achieve the allied parent's goals and objectives.

> **Allied Parent:** "It's not me, it the child who… (doesn't want to go on visitations with the targeted parent; doesn't want to accept phone calls from the targeted parent, wants to attend a particular school, etc.). I encourage the child to go on visitations (accept phone calls, etc.), but what can I do, I can't *force* the child to go."

ACS-11: "Deserves" to be Rejected. The child (and the allied parent) present a theme that the targeted parent "deserves" to be rejected because of some parental failure.

ACS-12: Disregard of Court Orders. The allied parent frequently disregards Court orders and the authority of the Court, and the child may also then display a similar disregard for Court orders and Court authority (possibly evidenced in threats to run away or in actual runaway behavior from the care of the targeted parent in defiance of Court orders for visitation and custody).

Treatment-Focused Assessment

A child's rejection of a parent is a treatment-related issue, not a child custody issue. A child rejecting a parent represents an attachment pathology called "pathological mourning" (Bowlby, 1980).[23] A treatment-focused assessment should be directed toward addressing the treatment-related needs of the child and family that are required to restore the child's normal-range and healthy development. Child custody decisions assess whether either parent represents a danger to the child and custody decisions focus on establishing the custody time-share schedule for the child's time with each parent. Resolving a child's rejection of a parent, on the other hand, is a treatment-related issue, not necessarily a custody-related issue.

In the absence of danger to the child from child abuse, there is no information in the scientific or theoretical literature that would allow professional psychology to render an opinion on the relative benefits from a 60-40% custody time-share relative to a 70-30% custody time-share, compared to an 80-20% custody time-share, as opposed to a 90-10% custody time-share, or as compared to a 50-50% custody time-share for any specific case. The relevant factors are far too complex to allow for such fine-grained determinations in any specific case. The only scientifically and theoretically supported custody time-share recommendation that can be supported by the scientific and theoretical literature on child development and parent-child relationships is that children benefit from a complex relationship with both parents. Therefore, based on the foundational principle that children benefit from a complex relationship with both parents, the only scientifically and theoretically supported recommendation from professional psychology regarding child custody would be for a 50-50% custody time-share schedule (except in cases of child abuse where a parent presents a danger to the child).

Parents may cooperatively decide on an alternative time-share schedule of shared custody, and alternative time-share schedules can be fully appropriate and healthy for the child. The issue is only that there is

---

[23] Bowlby, J. (1980). Attachment and loss: Vol. 3. Loss: Sadness and depression. NY: Basic Books.

no scientifically or theoretically supported information that would allow professional psychology to render a professionally responsible and supported opinion regarding the relative benefits of differing time-share schedules in any specific case, other than in cases of child abuse when the parent presents a danger to the child.

Does that mean that mental health professionals cannot render an opinion regarding the relative benefits of different custody time-share alternatives in any specific case? People can develop and render opinions about a wide array of topics. That does not, however, mean that these opinions are supported by the scientific and theoretical evidence. Regarding parenting, child development, and custody time-share alternatives, in the absence of child abuse, there is no the scientifically or theoretically supported basis that would allow professional psychology to render an opinion on the relative benefits to be derived from a 60-40% custody time-share relative to a 70-30% custody time-share, compared to an 80-20% custody time-share, as opposed to a 90-10% custody time-share, or compared to a 50-50% custody time-share for any specific case. Any opinion offered would simply be a matter of personal conjecture by an individual without any supporting foundation in the scientific and theoretical literature of professional psychology.

In the absence of scientifically or theoretically supported information regarding the relative benefits in any individual case of differing custody time-share alternatives, the only professionally supported recommendation from professional psychology in all cases of child custody (in the absence of child abuse) would be for a 50-50% custody time-share schedule based on the foundationally supported principle that children benefit from a complex relationship with both parents (except in cases of child abuse where a child protection response is warranted). Pathogenic parenting that is creating significant psychopathology in the child is a case of child protection concerns that might have child custody implications. Custody-related decisions relative to pathogenic parenting and child protection considerations should be data-driven by the treatment needs of the child and family. If the child is evidencing documented symptoms associated with the pathogenic parenting by one parent, then a treatment-related adjustment to the custody time-share schedule may needed to decrease the child's exposure to the distorted parenting practices of the pathogenic parent and increase the child's exposure to the healthier parenting of the normal-range parent. These decisions, however, should be data-driven based on the documented increase or decrease in the child's symptoms.

A child rejecting a parent is an attachment related pathology. The attachment system never spontaneously dysfunctions. It ONLY becomes dysfunctional in response to pathogenic parenting. Pathogenic parenting is a treatment-related issue. Resolving the attachment-related pathology of a child rejecting a parent requires a treatment-focused assessment, not a custody evaluation. In cases of disputed custody and inter-spousal conflict, a treatment-focused need of the family would consider a child custody schedule set at 50-50% to be the most advantageous treatment consideration in order to avoid making the child a "custody prize" to be won in the inter-spousal conflict, and based on the foundational principle that children benefit from a complex relationship with both parents. A treatment-focused assessment should then be conducted to identify the source of the pathogenic parenting that is creating the child's attachment-related pathology that would lead to a written treatment plan for resolving the family's problematic parenting that leads to the child's attachment-related pathology.

A targeted *Treatment-Focused Assessment Protocol* (Appendix 2) can be conducted across six to eight clinical interview sessions with the family members to identify the source of the pathogenic parenting creating the child's attachment-related pathology. The assessment protocol should directly assess for the presence or absence of the three diagnostic indicators and the 12 Associated Clinical Signs of attachment-based "parental alienation" AB-PA using the *Diagnostic Checklist for Pathogenic Parenting* (Appendix 4). The assessment protocol should also assess the parenting of the targeted-rejected parent using the *Parenting Practices Rating Scale* (Appendix 5) in order to establish that the parenting practices of the targeted parent are broadly normal-range as a qualifying condition of diagnostic indicator 1, or alternatively to specifically identify the parenting practices of the targeted-rejected parent that are of concern. The construct of normal-range parenting should be interpreted within the context of the general parenting practices evidenced within society, with due consideration given to cultural values and to the legitimate rights and prerogatives of parents for establishing family values through their use of normal-range discipline practices. In general, normal-range parenting on the *Parenting Practices Rating Scale* would be parenting in Categories 3 and 4, and a Permissive-to-Structured rating between 25 and 75.

The six to eight treatment-focused assessment sessions are structured into three phases, an initial phase with each parent individually, a direct assessment phase of the parent-child(ren) relationship, and a concluding assessment of parental schemas for responding to and organizing the information from the assessment.

The Initial Phase: An initial 90-minute assessment session is conducted with each parent individually to collect history and symptom information, and to obtain each parent's perception regarding the child and the family issues of concern. Additional initial parent sessions can be conducted for particularly complex family histories.

Direct Assessment Phase: The next phase of the assessment occurs in joint sessions with the child(ren) and the targeted-rejected parent to directly observe the parent-child(ren) relationship and the symptoms evidenced by the child(ren).

During these direct assessment sessions, response-to-intervention probes of the parent-child relationship can help illuminate the nature and severity of parent-child symptoms. Individual child sessions with an older child can also be conducted to more fully explore this child's perspective, but at least one joint parent-child(ren) assessment session with the targeted parent and child(ren) should be conducted to directly observe and assess the symptom display.

Parental Schema Assessment: The final phase of the treatment-focused assessment is to meet again individually with each parent and provide each parent with feedback regarding the assessment of symptoms in order to evaluate the parental schemas[24] for organizing this information.

Child Psychological Abuse

Pathogenic parenting that is creating significant developmental pathology in the child (diagnostic indicator 1), personality disorder pathology in the child or phobic anxiety pathology in the child (diagnostic indicator 2), and a delusional-psychiatric pathology in the child (diagnostic indicator 3) represents a DSM-5[25] diagnosis of V995.51 Child Psychological Abuse, Confirmed. The full DSM-5 diagnosis for the pathology of AB-PA is:

<u>DSM-5 Diagnosis</u>

309.4 Adjustment Disorder with mixed disturbance of emotions and conduct

V61.20 Parent-Child Relational Problem

V61.29 Child Affected by Parental Relationship Distress

V995.51 Child Psychological Abuse, Confirmed (pathogenic parenting)

In all cases of child abuse, physical child abuse, sexual child abuse, and psychological child abuse, the first obligation is to protect the child.

---

[24] Beck et al., (2004): "How a situation is evaluated depends in part, at least, on the relevant underlying beliefs. These beliefs are embedded in more or less stable structures, labeled "schemas," that select and synthesize incoming data." (p. 17)
Beck, A.T., Freeman, A., Davis, D.D., & Associates (2004). Cognitive therapy of personality disorders. (2nd edition). New York: Guilford.
[25] American Psychiatric Association. (2013). Diagnostic and statistical manual of mental disorders (Revised 5th ed.). Washington, DC: Author.

Protective Separation: In all cases of child abuse, physical child abuse, sexual child abuse, and psychological child abuse, the standard of practice and professional "duty to protect" requires the child's protective separation from the abusive parent.

Restoration of Healthy Development: In all cases of child abuse, physical child abuse, sexual child abuse, and psychological child abuse, the damage to the child's emotional and psychological development created by the abuse is then treated, and the child's healthy emotional and psychological development is restored.

Collateral Therapy: In cases of child abuse, it is strongly recommended that the abusive parent be required to obtain collateral individual therapy to gain and demonstrate insight into the causes of the prior abusive parenting practices.

Reintroducing the Formerly Abusive Parent: In most cases of child abuse, once the child's normal-range and healthy development has been recovered and stabilized, the child's relationship with the formerly abusive parent is reintroduced with sufficient safeguards to ensure that the child abuse does not resume once the relationship with the formerly abusive parent is reintroduced. The degree of parental cooperation with collateral therapy demonstrated by the formerly abusive parent, and this parent's demonstrated insight into the causes of the prior abusive parenting, are typically used as determining factors in the level of subsequent safeguards needed to protect the child.

3 Strategic Family Systems Intervention

Traditional Family Therapy

The standard family systems treatment for a cross-generational coalition of the child with one parent against the other parent is to bring this hidden form of pathology into the open and have the allied parent's covert but pervasive negative influence on the child openly acknowledged. The goal is to help the allied parent develop insight into the alliance, and then to activate this parent's empathy for the child's authentic experience of loving both parents. This leads to the parent's understanding for the damaging effects on the child from the child's triangulation into the spousal conflict, with the goal of engaging the allied parent's *cooperation* in releasing the child from the cross-generational coalition.

However, many allied parents may resist acknowledging the coalition with the child, as indicated in Jay Haley's definition of the cross-generational coalition;

"The coalition between the two persons is denied. That is, there is certain behavior which indicates a coalition which, when it is queried, will be denied as a coalition." (Haley, 1977, p. 37)

This is especially true when the allied parent's own psychological self-interest is heavily invested in the child's role as a *"regulatory object"* in stabilizing the emotional and psychological state of the parent. A parent who has prominent **abandonment fears** or feels a **vengeful hostility** directed toward the other spouse/parent may be extracting his or her own psychological stability from the child's rejection of the other parent;

Psychological Process: "I'm not the abandoned (spouse)/parent; you are. See, the child is rejecting you and choosing me. I'm not the flawed and inadequate (spouse)/parent; you are. The child is rejecting you because of your inadequacy as a (spouse)/parent, and the child is choosing me because I'm the wonderful and ideal (spouse)/parent."

If the allied parent has a strong psychological investment in maintaining the child's symptomatic hostility toward the other parent (toward the other spouse), then the allied parent will steadfastly deny the existence of the coalition and will continually place the child out front as supposedly making an *"independent decision"* to reject the other parent. This is called a **"role-reversal"** relationship in which the child is being used by the parent to meet the parent's own emotional and psychological needs (in this case to meet the parent's **spousal** need for revenge against the other spouse for the divorce, and/or the **spousal** need to dispel personal fears of abandonment triggered by the divorce). When the allied parent resists developing insight and steadfastly denies the cross-generational coalition with the child despite the child's symptomatic behavior that is clearly evident of the coalition, then an alternative treatment approach is needed that will effectively release the child from being *triangulated* into the spousal conflict by the emotional and psychological needs of the allied parent.

When a cross-generational coalition is present, treatment must first protect the child. Treatment efforts that seek to restore the child's affectionate bond to the targeted parent without first protecting the child from the psychological pressures and potential psychological retaliation placed on the child by the allied parent in the cross-generational coalition with the child will simply turn the child into a **psychological battleground** between the efforts of therapy to restore a normal-range parent-child relationship with the targeted parent and the continuing efforts of the allied parent to create and maintain the child's symptomatic rejection of the targeted parent. Turning the child into a psychological battleground between the efforts of therapy to restore normal-range bonding with the targeted parent and the efforts of the allied parent to keep the child symptomatically rejecting of the targeted parent will be psychologically damaging to the child. Therapy for a cross-generational coalition that does not involve the active cooperation of the allied parent in releasing the child from the coalition will require that we first protect the child from the pathogenic parental influence of the allied parent who is creating and maintaining the child's symptomatic rejection of the other parent.

Treatment that does not involve the voluntary release of the child from the parent-child coalition with the allied pathogenic parent will likely require that the child first be protectively separated from the pathogenic parenting of the allied parent during the active phase of the child's treatment and recovery stabilization. The professional rationale for the protective separation period from the pathogenic parenting of the allied parent is based on a confirmed DSM-5 diagnosis of V995.51 Child Psychological Abuse that warrants a child protection response.

However, a treatment-related alternative to a protective separation may be available from a Strategic family systems intervention of a *Contingent Visitation Schedule* that is designed to extract the child from being triangulated into the inter-spousal conflict by altering the power conferred by the child's symptoms within the family's relationships, which will then free the child from the cross-generational coalition created by the allied pathogenic parent. The Strategic family systems intervention of a *Contingent Visitation Schedule* can be used as a Response-to-Intervention trial preceding the application of a protective separation period to assess whether a protective separation is needed, or whether a less impactful intervention can resolve the family pathology, or the Strategic family systems intervention of a *Contingent Visitation Schedule* can be used following the child's protective separation and recovery of normal-range development in order to protect the child from the continuing pathogenic parenting of the allied parent once contact with this parent is restored.

Strategic Family Therapy: The Symptom Confers Power

Strategic family systems therapy (principle theorists: Jay Haley; Chloe Madanes) is one of two primary schools of family systems therapy generally, the other being Structural family systems therapy (principle theorist: Salvador Minuchin). All family systems models rely on similar basic foundational principles regarding the functioning and dysfunctioning of family systems, with the differences between various approaches typically being a difference in emphasis or differing techniques used to achieve common goals. A foundational emphasis of Strategic family systems therapy is the recognition that the symptom confers power within the family, and the goal of Strategic family systems therapy is to identify how the symptom is conferring power and to then change this power dynamic within the family in such a way that the symptom ceases to provide this power. Once the symptom no longer serves its role in conferring power within the family system, the symptom will lose its function within family relationships and it will drop away.

In the family pathology of a *cross-generational coalition*, the child's symptomatic hostility toward the targeted-rejected parent confers power to the allied parent in the following ways:

- **Confers Power to Expresses Spousal Anger:** In the pathology of the cross-generational coalition, the child's induced anger toward the targeted parent is being created and used by the allied parent to divert the **spousal** anger of the allied parent toward the other **spouse** through the child. The anger toward the targeted parent that is created in the child by the pathogenic parenting of the allied parent allows the allied parent to indirectly express this parent's own **spousal** anger toward the other **spouse** by essentially "weaponizing" and using the child in the inter-spousal conflict. Through the pathogenic parenting of the allied parent, the child becomes a proxy warrior for the allied parent in this parent's conflict with the other spouse. The allied parent in the cross-generational coalition uses the child's induced anger and rejection of the other spouse/(parent) to exact a retaliatory revenge on the other spouse surrounding the divorce by creating conflict, pain, and suffering in the other spouse-and-parent through the covertly created and covertly supported parent-child conflict created by the pathogenic parenting of the allied parent.

- **Confers Power to Dispel Abandonment Fears:** The child's rejection of the targeted parent acts to define the targeted parent (the other spouse) as being the "abandoned" and "rejected" parent (spouse), while the child's displayed bonding to the allied and supposedly "favored" parent defines this parent (spouse) as the all-wonderful, never-to-be abandoned parent (spouse). By creating conflict between the child and the other parent that prevents the child from forming a bonded relationship with the other parent, the allied and supposedly "favored" parent is able to dispel his or her own abandonment fears caused by the divorce by projecting and displacing the abandonment onto the other parent - "I'm not the abandoned and rejected parent/(spouse); you are."

- **Confers Power to Restore the Narcissistic Defense:** The grandiose and idealized presentation of the narcissistic personality as being the "all-wonderful" person/parent/spouse is a defense against deeper feelings of primal self-inadequacy. The rejection by the other spouse surrounding the divorce penetrated the allied parent's narcissistic defense against deep-seated feelings of core self-inadequacy, causing a collapse of the narcissistic parent's personality structure into profoundly painful feelings of self-inadequacy. In order to restore the narcissistic defense, the allied narcissistic parent creates and then exploits the child's rejection of the other parent/(spouse) to define the other parent/(spouse) as the inadequate and rejected person, which reestablishes the narcissistic self-image of idealized magnificence and superiority that was damaged by the rejection surrounding divorce – "I'm not the inadequate and rejected parent/(spouse); you are. The child is choosing me and rejecting you because it's you who is the inadequate person/parent/(spouse), while I'm the ideal and perfect parent/person/(spouse)."

- **Confers Power to Nullify Court Orders for Custody:** The allied parent in the cross-generational coalition with the child exploits the child's induced hostility and rejection of the targeted parent to nullify Court orders for custody and visitation and obtain sole custody possession of the child behind the cover of the child's supposedly "independent decision" to reject the other parent. By "weaponizing" the child through powerful (yet covert) techniques of psychological manipulation and psychological control, and then claiming that the child's rejection of the other parent is the "independent decision" made by the child, the allied parent is able to hide his or her psychological control of the child behind assertions that it is the child's own supposedly "independent decision" to reject the other parent that is resulting the disruption to the Court-ordered custody and visitation schedule. The typical role-reversal exploitative refrain offered by the allied parent is:

    > **Allied Parent:** "It's not me, it's the child who is refusing visitations with the other parent. I encourage the child to go on visitations, but what can I do? I can't *force* the child to go."

This refrain of putting the child out-front and then exploiting the child's (induced) rejection of the other parent is often accompanied by efforts to **empower** the child's ability to reject the other parent:

> **Allied Parent:** "The child should decide on whether to go on visitations with the other parent. We should listen to what the child wants. The child should be allowed to testify and speak with the judge about what the child wants."

First the allied parent creates the child's hostility and rejection of the targeted parent through coercive parenting practices of psychological manipulation and psychological control, and then the allied parent seeks to *exploit* the child's induced symptomatic rejection of the other parent to nullify Court orders for custody and visitation. As this process progresses, the allied parent increasingly seeks to *empower* the child's ability to reject the other parent. By hiding behind the child's induced pathology of rejecting the other parent, the allied parent in a cross-generational coalition with the child seeks to gain sole custody possession of the child, irrespective of the child's authentic love toward the other parent, irrespective of the parental rights of the other parent, and irrespective of Court orders for shared custody and visitation. The child's symptom confers power to the allied parent to nullify Court orders for shared custody and visitation and obtain sole custody possession of the child.

The Strategic Family Systems intervention must therefore alter the following features of how the child's hostility and rejection of the targeted parent confers power to the allied parent:

1) **Spousal Anger:** The child's symptoms are used to express spousal anger toward the targeted parent and exact a retaliatory revenge on the targeted parent for the divorce;

2) **Abandonment Fears:** The child's symptoms are used to dispel the allied parents own abandonment fears by defining the targeted parent as the rejected and abandoned parent/(spouse)

3) **Narcissistic Defense:** The child's symptoms are used to restore the narcissistic defense of the allied parent by defining the targeted parent as the inadequate person/parent/(spouse) and the allied parent as the all-wonderful and ideal parent/person/(spouse);

4) **Nullify Court Orders:** The child's symptoms are used to nullify Court orders for shared custody and visitation by hiding behind and exploiting the child's induced rejection of the targeted parent.

The Strategic family system intervention needs to eliminate all of these power components surrounding the child's symptomatic rejection of the targeted parent, so that instead of the child's symptoms of hostility and rejection conferring power to the allied parent in the cross-generational coalition, the child's symptoms must instead, through the intervention, confer power to the other parent, to the currently targeted-rejected parent. This will require assigning the proper attribution of causality for the child's symptoms to the pathogenic parenting of the allied parent who has formed a cross-generational coalition with the child against the other parent through psychologically coercive parenting practices of manipulation and the psychological control of the child.

Contingent Visitation Schedule

A Strategic family systems treatment intervention of a *Contingent Visitation Schedule* that appropriately holds the pathogenic parenting of the allied parent responsible for the child's symptom display of hostility and rejection of the targeted parent can alter and reverse the power dynamic being conferred by the child's symptomatic rejection of the targeted parent. The development and implementation of a treatment-related *Contingent Visitation Schedule* should be based on the findings from a Treatment-Focused Assessment, the subsequent DSM-5 diagnosis, and the case conceptualization based on the assessment and diagnosis, consistent with the foundational principles of clinical psychology that assessment leads to diagnosis, and diagnosis then guides treatment.

Child Custody: The treatment-related recommendation for the Court ordered child custody visitation schedule within the *Contingent Visitation Schedule* is for a shared 50-50% custody visitation time-share, preferably a one-week-on/one-week-off schedule. Children benefit from a complex relationship with both parents, and a shared 50-50% custody time-share provides the child with the opportunity to develop a healthy and bonded relationship with both parents.

The Treatment Plan: The treatment for the child's display of increased symptoms of pathology is a structured flexibility in the visitation schedule that is responsive to the child's treatment-related needs, based on the attributed cause of the child's symptoms to the pathogenic parenting of the allied parent who has formed a cross-generational coalition with the child that is creating the child's pathology.

In the pre-treatment condition, the child's symptomatic hostility and rejection of the targeted parent <u>reduces</u> the targeted parent's custody and visitation time with the child, and in doing so confers power to the allied parent in a cross-generational coalition with the child to gain sole possession of the child. Since the cause of the child's pathology is located in the pathogenic parenting of the allied parent who has formed a cross-generational coalition with the child against the targeted parent, the treatment-related intervention is to make the child's involvement with the pathogenic parenting of the allied parent contingent upon the child remaining non-symptomatic. If the pathogenic parenting of the allied parent creates pathology in the child, then the amount of time the child is exposed to the pathogenic parenting of the allied parent is reduced, and the amount of time the child spends with the targeted parent is <u>increased</u> in order to repair the damage created in their relationship by the pathogenic parenting of the allied parent. This represents an appropriate treatment-related response to the causal origins for the child's pathology.

Altering the Power Dynamic:

By appropriately locating the causal attribution for the child's pathology in the pathogenic parenting of the allied parent, a symptom-contingent intervention will eliminate the power being conferred to the pathogenic allied parent by the child's symptoms.

1. **Disrupting the Expression of Spousal Anger:** In the pre-treatment family system, the spousal anger of the allied parent is being diverted through the child by using the child's covertly created hostility and rejection toward the targeted parent as a weapon to inflict conflict and distress onto the other spouse/parent. With the *Contingent Visitation Schedule*, however, the targeted parent is now also being "rewarded" when the child is symptomatic by granting more child time to the targeted parent as compensation for the more difficult parenting task of repairing the parent-child relationship that is being damaged by the pathogenic parenting of the allied parent. The child's symptoms, while still hostile and punitive toward the targeted parent, are also now being counter-balanced by the positive "reward" the targeted parent receives of increased parent-child time needed to repair the damage to the parent-child relationship being caused by the pathogenic parenting of the allied parent.

2. **Preventing the Displacement of Abandonment Fears:** In the pre-treatment condition, the child's symptoms and pathology resulted in increased child time with the allied parent that serves to dispel the allied parent's own fears of abandonment by projectively displacing these fears onto the other parent ("I'm not the rejected and abandoned parent/person/(spouse), you are."). The *Contingent Visitation Schedule* negates this ability of the child's symptoms to dispel the allied parent's abandonment fears by reducing rather than increasing the allied parent's time with the child in response to the child symptoms. By reducing rather than increasing the allied parent's time with the child in response to the child's symptomatic behavior, the child's symptoms will no longer result in a reduction to the allied parent's fears of being abandoned, and will actually increase any fears of abandonment. By reducing the allied parent's time with the child in response to the creation of child symptoms, the child's symptoms become counter-productive for the allied parent by actually increasing any abandonment fears this parent may have that were previously being resolved by the child's symptomatic rejection of the other parent.

3. **Undermining the Restoration of the Narcissistic Defense:** By holding the allied parent responsible for creating the child's symptoms, the child's symptoms no longer serve their function of defining the targeted parent as being the "bad parent" and the allied parent as being idealized "good parent." Instead,

through the treatment response of the *Contingent Visitation Schedule*, the emergence of child symptoms subjects the allied parent to negative evaluation as being the problematic parent, which then disrupts the ability of the child's symptoms to restore the allied parent's narcissistic defense as the supposedly ideal and all-wonderful "good parent."

4. **Preventing the Nullification of Court Orders:** Within the *Contingent Visitation Schedule*, the Court's orders for child custody are for a shared 50-50% custody time-share based on the foundational principle that children benefit from a complex relationship with both parents. The *Contingent Visitation Schedule* prevents the allied parent from manipulatively creating pathology in the child as a means to nullify Court orders for shared custody visitation by appropriately attributing the child's pathology to the pathogenic parenting practices of the allied parent who has formed a cross-generational coalition with the child against the targeted parent (based on the prior mental health assessment and the case conceptualization). Within the treatment-related response of the *Contingent Visitation Schedule*, the allied parent is held appropriately responsible for ensuring that Court orders for shared child custody and visitation are followed, and the ability of the allied parent to create-and-exploit the child's pathology as a means to nullify Court orders for shared parental custody is eliminated. Within the treatment-related response of the *Contingent Visitation Schedule*, attempts by the allied parent to nullify Court orders for shared custody and visitation by creating pathology in the child are immediately addressed as treatment-related issues, the targeted parent is granted more custody time to repair the parent-child relationship being damaged by the pathogenic parenting of the allied parent, and the child's exposure to the pathogenic parenting of the allied parent that is creating the child's pathology is reduced until the child's symptoms are resolved.

Responsibility for Creating Child Pathology

Treatment of attachment-related child pathology begins with an assessment regarding the cause of the child's symptoms. Since the attachment system <u>never</u> spontaneously dysfunctions, but ONLY becomes dysfunctional in response to pathogenic parenting, the purpose of the initial assessment is to identify the source of the pathogenic parenting that is creating the child's attachment-related pathology. If an appropriate Treatment-Focused Assessment identifies that the allied parent has formed a cross-generational coalition with the child against the other parent, then the pathogenic parenting of the allied parent is responsible for the child's symptomatic hostility and rejection of the targeted parent.

In response to this diagnostic determination of parental responsibility in creating the child's pathology, the treatment-related response of the *Contingent Visitation Schedule* places appropriate responsibility for the creation of the child's hostility and attachment-related symptoms toward the targeted parent on the distorted and pathogenic parenting practices of the allied parent. Within the pathology of a cross-generational coalition, the allied parent seeks to hide and avoid responsibility for creating the child's hostility and conflict with the other parent behind the claim that the child's rejection of the other parent is the child's own "independent decision." However, when an appropriate Treatment-Focused Assessment of the child and family pathology identifies a cross-generational coalition as the cause of the child's symptoms (through the various diagnostic features of the child's and family's symptom display), the *Contingent Visitation Schedule* appropriately disallows the attempt by the allied parent to hide parental responsibility for creating the child's pathology by the false assertion that it is the child's "independent decision" when the child's thoughts and feelings are actually the product of the manipulative psychological control and pathogenic parental influence exerted on the child by the allied pathogenic parent.

When an appropriate *Treatment-Focused Assessment* has determined that the child's symptoms are being created through a cross-generational coalition with the allied parent, the required treatment response to child displays of symptomatic behavior toward the targeted parent is to attribute causal responsibility for the child's symptoms to the distorted and manipulative parenting of the allied parent. Increased child treatment time with the targeted parent is then required to undo the effects of the distorted parenting of the allied parent, and decreased child time with the allied parent is required to minimize the negative impact of the allied parent's negative parenting on the child.

The *Contingent Visitation Schedule* is a treatment-related intervention needed to counteract the negative pathogenic parenting practices of the allied parent who is forming a cross-generational coalition with the child against the other parent/(spouse). If the child's behavior with the targeted parent is broadly normal-range (as assessed by the treating family therapist, and documented in parental ratings), then the custody and visitation schedule is for a shared 50-50% custody timeshare schedule. If, however, the child evidences a prominent rise in symptomatic behavior as a presumed consequence of the cross-generational coalition and distorted pathogenic parenting of the allied parent (based on the assessment, diagnosis, and case conceptualization of the child's symptoms), then the treatment-related intervention of the *Contingent Visitation Schedule* is implemented to treat the child's symptomatic behavior being created by the distorted parenting of the allied parent.

Treatment-Related Impact of the Contingent Visitation Schedule

Removing the Child from the Loyalty Conflict

The *Contingent Visitation Schedule* removes the child from the middle of the "loyalty conflict" created by the distorted parenting of the allied parent in a cross-generational coalition of the child against the other parent. In the pre-treatment condition, the child is showing "loyalty" to the allied parent in the cross-generational coalition by rejecting the targeted parent. The *Contingent Visitation Schedule* changes this loyalty situation for the child. Under the *Contingent Visitation Schedule*, the child is allowed to show "loyalty" to the allied parent (i.e., a desire to spend more time with the allied parent) by NOT misbehaving with the targeted parent, since by <u>not</u> misbehaving with the targeted parent the child is able to spend more time with the allied parent.

This allows the child to bond to the targeted parent (show loyalty to the targeted parent) as the means to spend more time with the allied parent (show loyalty to the allied parent). The structure of the *Contingent Visitation Schedule* removes the child from the "loyalty bind" created by the cross-generational coalition of having to choose one or the other parent in the *spousal* dispute.

Reversing the Power Dynamic

By making the child's time with the allied parent contingent upon the child's <u>positive behavior</u> with the currently targeted-rejected parent, the *Contingent Visitation Schedule* reverses the power dynamic conferred by the child's symptomatic hostility and rejection of the targeted-rejected parent. Instead of the child's symptoms reducing the targeted parent's time with the child and conferring more custody time to the allied parent who is creating the child's rejection of the other parent, under the *Contingent Visitation Schedule* the child's symptomatic behavior **reduces** the custody and visitation time of the **allied parent** who is responsible for creating the child's symptomatic rejection of the other parent, and "rewards" the targeted parent with more child time. The child's symptoms cease to confer the power of providing more custody time to the allied parent who is creating the child's symptoms.

The child's symptoms that are created by the psychological control and manipulation of the child by the allied pathogenic parent also no longer nullify Court orders for custody and visitation by creating a de facto sole custody to the allied parent. When the child's symptoms no longer confer the functional power to the allied parent to nullify Court orders for child custody and obtain de facto sole custody possession of the child -

irrespective of Court orders for shared custody and irrespective of the parental rights of the other parent - then the allied parent's motivation to create the child's symptomatic rejection of the other parent diminishes.

Furthermore, since the *Contingent Visitation Schedule* <u>decreases</u> the <u>allied</u> parent's time with the child for displays of child symptoms, the child's symptoms no longer act to reduce the allied parent's abandonment fears. Instead, the child's symptoms actually increase any existing fears of abandonment of the allied parent, placing further motivational pressure on the allied parent to NOT create the child's symptomatic rejection of the other parent. Under the *Contingent Visitation Schedule*, the child's symptoms are also "rewarding" the targeted parent with increased time with the child, which is contrary to the revenge motivations of the allied parent, thereby further reducing the function of spousal revenge being served in creating the child's symptomatic rejection of the targeted parent.

Data-Driven Decision Making

Within the *Contingent Visitation Schedule*, decisions about custody and visitation time-share are made based on data regarding the child's symptoms (daily ratings on the *Parent-Child Relationship Rating Scale*; reviewed weekly with the Organizing Family Therapist; Appendix 6).

If the child's symptomatic behavior increases toward the targeted parent as assessed and documented by daily ratings on the *Parent-Child Relationship Rating Scale*, then the child visitation time with the targeted parent is increased in order to allow for the treatment-related resolution of the parent-child conflict created by the cross-generational coalition of the child with the allied parent (as determined by prior assessment, diagnosis, and case conceptualization). When the child's symptomatic behavior decreases and the child's behavior returns to a normal-range, then contact with the pathogenic parenting of the allied parent who is covertly creating the child's symptoms through aberrant and distorted parenting of psychological control and manipulation (as determined by assessment, diagnosis, and the organizing case conceptualization) is resumed.

Decisions are data-driven based on the child's symptoms, and are housed within an overarching case conceptualization based on prior assessment and diagnosis of the family's relationship patterns. The child's exposure to the *pathogenic parenting* of the allied parent who is creating the child's pathology is made contingent upon the degree of child pathology being created and expressed by the child, as documented daily using the *Parent-Child Relationship Rating Scale*, and subject to weekly therapist monitoring and review.

Structuring the Contingent Visitation Schedule:

The monitoring and implementation of the treatment-related *Contingent Visitation Schedule* is the responsibility of an Organizing Family Therapist who is assigned to oversee the treatment of the family. The Organizing Family Therapist is responsible for the following functions in the management of the *Contingent Visitation Schedule*:

1. **Establishing Criteria:** The Organizing Family Therapist is responsible for determining the rating scale criteria for a child's "Successful Day" with the targeted parent and the achievement of a "Successful Week." Generally, a "Successful Day" is considered to be a rating of 4 or higher on all three primary relationship scales, 1) Child Attitude, 2) Child Cooperation, and 3) Child Sociability of the *Parent-Child Relationship Rating Scale* (Appendix 6). Adjusting the criteria definition for a "Successful Day" (such a lowering the criteria during the early phases of treatment and increasing the expectations as treatment and recovery progresses) should be at the sole discretion of the Organizing Family Therapist.

2. **Fidelity Monitoring of Ratings:** The Organizing Family Therapist is responsible for monitoring the fidelity of the child ratings by the targeted parent to ensure the accuracy and reliability of these parental ratings through discussions with the targeted parent and child(ren) during weekly family therapy sessions, in

which problematic child behavior is reviewed and the parental response is discussed. These family therapy discussions of ratings should produce a clear consensus on expectations for appropriate child behavior and rating criteria.

3. **Implementing the *Contingent Visitation Schedule*:** It is the responsibility of the Organizing Family Therapist to determine whether the weekly criteria for shared 50-50% custody have been met or whether the child's symptoms have triggered the need to implement the *Contingent Visitation Schedule*.

   The decision to implement the treatment-related *Contingent Visitation Schedule* should be at the sole discretion of the Organizing Family Therapist, based on the degree of child symptoms documented by the *Parent-Child Relationship Rating Scale* and the treatment criteria definition for child behavior expectations.

   Ending a period of the treatment-related *Contingent Visitation Schedule* should similarly be at the sole discretion of the Organizing Family Therapist, based on the degree of child symptoms documented by the *Parent-Child Relationship Rating Scale* and the criteria definition for child behavior expectations.

   Treatment-related decisions surrounding the implementation and ending of periods of the Contingent Visitation Schedule should rely on the defined criteria and requirements for "Successful Days" based on symptom documentation using the Parent-Child Relationship Rating Scale. The Organizing Family Therapist has the authority to override the ratings made by the targeted parent if, in the clinical judgement of the Organizing Family Therapist and after discussion in family therapy, it is the opinion of the Organizing Family Therapist that the ratings of the targeted parent do not accurately reflect the actual child behavior during that period.

Example Criteria Definitions:

Successful Day: The child receives a rating of 4 or higher on all three relationship rating items, 1) Hostility-Affection, 2) Defiance-Cooperation, and 3) Withdrawal-Sociability on the *Parent-Child Relationship Rating Scale*.

Successful Week (week-on/week off visitation schedule): The child has had five Successful Days during the seven-day week period.

Unsuccessful Week (week-on/week off visitation schedule): The child has had fewer than five Successful Days during the seven-day period; triggering the Short-Term Contingent Visitation Response.

Short-Term Contingent Visitation Response: The child remains in the custody care of the targeted parent and must receive three consecutive Successful Days before a return to standard 50-50% custody visitation time-share is resumed. Days spent with the targeted parent are lost to the allied parent, with no make-up days, and standard transfer days are resumed once the 50-50% schedule is resumed.

Serious Breech: The child evidences a serious behavior of professional concern, such as runaway behavior or physical aggression; triggering Long-Term Contingent Visitation Response.

Long-Term Contingent Visitation Response: The child remains in the care of the targeted parent for two additional Successful Weeks. In addition, the child must have three Successful Days in the final three days before ending of the Long-Term Contingent Visitation Response. Days spent with the targeted parent are lost to the allied parent, with no make-up days, and standard transfer days are resumed once the 50-50% schedule is resumed.

Phone and Text Contact: Each parent is allowed the following phone and text contact with the child during their non-custodial week.

> **Daily:** One morning greeting text exchange and one evening bedtime text exchange with the child, not to exceed five individual messages from the parent and five individual messages from the child that are of

reasonable length and appropriate content (the Organizing Family Therapist can monitor texts for appropriate length and content, if warranted). The child is expected to provide at least one initial response text to the parent, and all texts should evidence appropriate social-skills.

Weekly (week-on/week-off visitation schedule): One mid-week telephone call of 30 minutes. One end-week telephone call of 30 minutes. For example, if the exchange is weekly on Friday after school, then the mid-week call would be on Monday or Tuesday, and the late week Call would be on Wednesday or Thursday). Skype video calls can be substituted for phone calls at the discretion of the Organizing Family Therapist.

Skype: A daily 5 minute Skype goodnight video-call can be substituted for the bedtime text.

Parental Monitoring: Each parent has the right to be in the room during phone and Skype calls, as long as this parent does not intervene or intrude into the other parent's conversation with the child, and each parent has the right to review text messages sent and received to the child.

Optional Telephone/Text Refusal Modules:

Optional Intervention Modules are available to the Organizing Family Therapist to address an absence of appropriate social skills by the child during phone or text communication with the targeted parent, such as refusing to respond to text messages or refusing to accept mid-week or end-week phone calls.

Refusing Text Response: If the child refuses to respond with appropriate social skills to the targeted parent's morning or bedtime texts (or on the bedtime Skype call) on three occasions during the week, then the child spends two additional days with the targeted parent on the next visitation, and the final two days of this visitation period must be Successful Days before resuming the 50-50% custody schedule. These two Successful Days would be in addition to any additional program requirements for a Successful Week and the possible triggering of the *Contingent Visitation Schedule*. Triggering of the Refusing Text Response is at the discretion of the Organizing Family Therapist based on the description of the family events and the treatment-related concerns of the Organizing Family Therapist regarding the child's text-related behavior while in the custody of the allied parent.

Refusing Phone Calls: If the child refuses to accept or does not respond with appropriate social skills to the targeted parent's mid-week or end-week phone call during the week with the allied parent, then the child spends two additional days with the targeted parent on the next visitation period, and the final two days of this visitation period must be Successful Days before resuming the 50-50% custody schedule. These two Successful Days would be in addition to any additional program requirements for a Successful Week and the possible triggering of the *Contingent Visitation Schedule*. Triggering of the Refusing Phone Calls intervention is at the discretion of the Organizing Family Therapist based on the description of the family events and the treatment-related concerns of the Organizing Family Therapist for the child phone-related behavior.

Response to Intervention

It remains possible that even with the Strategic Family Systems intervention of a *Contingent Visitation Schedule*, the allied parent may nevertheless choose to sacrifice his or her own time with the child in order to continue creating the child's rejection of the other parent. If a six-month intervention with the *Contingent Visitation Schedule* does not result in significant improvement in the child's symptom display toward the targeted parent, as determined by data from the *Parent-Child Relationship Rating Scale* and appropriate assessment by the Organizing Family Therapist, then additional protective safeguards of the child's emotional and psychological development from the pathogenic parenting of the allied parent may be required. An increase to more significant levels of child protection should be based on the assessment, diagnosis, and case conceptualization of the Organizing Family Therapist following a six-month response to intervention period with the Strategic Family Systems Intervention of a *Contingent Visitation Schedule*.

Appendix 1: Research Studies on Parental Psychological Control of the Child Identified by Barber & Harmon (2002)

> Table 2-1: Overview of Studies Measuring Psychological Control (p. 29-32)
>
> From: Barber, B. K. (Ed.) (2002). Intrusive parenting: How psychological control affects children and adolescents. Washington, DC: American Psychological Association.

Teleki, J.K., Powell, J.A., & Claypool, P.L. (1984). Parental child rearing behavior perceived by parents and school-age children in divorced and married families. Home Economics Research Journal, 13, 41-51

Livotsky, V.G., & Dusek, J.B. (1985). Perceptions of child rearing and self-concept development during the early adolescent years. Journal of Youth and Adolescence, 14, 373-387.

Steinberg, L., Elmen, J.D., & Mounts, N.S. (1989). Authoritative parenting, psychosocial maturity, and academic success among adolescents. Child Development, 60, 1424-1436.

Eastburg, M., & Johnson, W.B., (1990). Shyness and perceptions of parental behavior. Psychological Reports, 66, 915-921.

Fauber, R., Forehand, R., Thomas, A.M., & Weirson, M. (1990). A mediational model of the impact of marital conflict on adolescent adjustment in intact and divorced families: The role of disrupted parenting. Child Development, 61, 1112-1123.

Barber, B.K., & Shagle, S.C. (1992). Adolescent problem behavior. A social ecological Analysis. Family Perspective, 26, 493-515.

Lyon, J.M., Henggeler, S., & Hall, J.A., (1992). The family relations, peer relations, and criminal activities of Caucasian and Hispanic-American gang members. Journal of Abnormal Child Psychology, 20, 439-449.

Forhand, R., & Nousiainen, S. (1993). Maternal and parental parenting: Critical dimensions to adolescent functioning. Journal of Family Psychology, 7, 213-221.

Shulman, S., Collins, W.A., & Dital, M. (1993). Parent-child relationships and peer-perceived competence during middle childhood and preadolescence in Israel. Journal of Early Adolescence, 13, 204-218.

Barber, B.K., Olsen, J.A., & Shagel, S. (1994). Associations between parental psychological control and behavior control and youth internalized and externalized behaviors. Child Development, 65, 1120-1136.

Bronstein, P. (1994). Patterns of parent-child interaction in Mexican families: A cross-cultural perspective. International Journal of Behavioral Development, 17, 423-446.

Comstock, D.C. (1994). Parental control and gender-specific etiology of internalized and externalized adolescent deviance. Master's thesis, Department of Sociology, Brigham Young University, Provo, Utah.

Imbimbo, P.V. (1995). Sex differences in the identity formation of college students from divorced families. Journal of Youth and Adolescence, 24, 745-761.

Barber B.K. (1996). Parental psychological control: Revisiting a neglected construct. Child Development, 67, 3296-3319.

Barber, B.K., & Olsen, J.A. (1997). Socialization in context: Connection, regulation, and autonomy in the family, school, and neighborhood, and with peers. Journal of Adolsescent Research, 12, 287-315

Bogenschneider, K., Small, S.A., & Tsay, J.C. (1997). Child, parent, and contextual influences on perceived parenting competence among parents of adolescents. Journal of Marriage and the Family, 59, 345-362.

Conger, K.J., Conger, R.D., & Scaramella, L.V. (1997). Parents, siblings, psychological control, and adolescent adjustment. Journal of Adolescent Research, 12, 113-138.

Garber, J., Robinson, N.S., & Valentiner, D. (1997). The relation between parenting and adolescent depression: Self-worth as a mediator. Journal of Adolescent Research, 12 12-33.

Jensen, B.S. (1997). Family interaction and adolescent female eating disorders: An analysis of family, marital, and parent-child level correlates. Master's thesis, Department of Sociology, Brigham Young University, Provo, Utah.

Litchfield, A.W., Thomas, D.L., & Li, B.D. (1997). Dimensions of religiosity as mediators of the relations between parenting and adolescent deviant behavior. Journal of Adolescent Research, 12, 199-226.

Bean, R.A. (1998). Academic grades, delinquency, and depression among ethnically diverse youth: The influences of parental support, behavioral control, and psychological control. Doctoral dissertation, Brigham Young University, Provo, Utah.

Hart, C.H., Nelson, D.A., Robinson, C.C., Olsen, S.F., & McNeilly-Choque, M.K., (1998). Overt and relational aggression in Russian nursery-school-age children: Parenting style and marital linkages. Developmental Psychology, 34, 687-697.

Knowlton, S.S. (1998). Connection, regulation, and autonomy: A comparison of nonclinical adolescents and adolescents in residential treatment. Master's thesis, Department of Family Sciences, Brigham Young University, Provo, Utah.

Mills, R.S.L., & Rubin, K.H. (1998). Are behavioural and psychological control both differentially associated with childhood aggression and social withdrawal? Canadian Journal of Behavioural Sciences, 30, 132-136

Wells, M.E.W. (1998). Psychological control and internalizing and externalizing behavior in early childhood. Master's thesis, Brigham Young University, Provo, Utah.

Barber, B.K. (1999). Political violence, family relations, and Palestinian youth functioning. Journal of Adolescent Research, 14, 206-230.

Pettit, G.S., Laird, R.D., Dodge, K.A., bates, J.E., & Criss, M.M. (2001). Antecedents and behavior-problem outcomes of parental monitoring and psychological control. Child Development, 72, 583-598.

Rodgers, K.B. (1999). Parenting processes related to sexual risk-taking behaviors of adolescent males and females. Journal of Marriage and the Family, 61, 99-109.

Morris, A.S., Steinberg, F.M., Sessa, S.A., Silk, J.S., & Essex, M. (2002) Measuring children's perceptions of psychological control: Developmental and conceptual considerations.. In B. K. Barber (Ed.), Intrusive parenting: How psychological control affects children and adolescents. Washington, DC: American Psychological Association.

Nelson, D.A., & Crick, N.R. (2002). Parental psychological control: Implications for childhood physical and relational aggression. In B. K. Barber (Ed.), Intrusive parenting: How psychological control affects children and adolescents. Washington, DC: American Psychological Association.

Olsen, S.F., Yang, C., Hart, C.H., Robinson, C.C., Wu, P., Nelson, D.A., Nelson, L.J., Jin, S., & Wo, J. (2002). Maternal psychological control and preschool children's behavioral outcomes in China, Russia, and the United States. In B. K. Barber (Ed.), Intrusive parenting: How psychological control affects children and adolescents. Washington, DC: American Psychological Association.

Pettit, G.S., & Laird, R.D. (2002). Psychological control and monitoring in early adolescence: The role of parental involvement and earlier child adjustment. In B. K. Barber (Ed.), Intrusive parenting: How psychological control affects children and adolescents. Washington, DC: American Psychological Association.

Holmbeck, G.N., Shapera, W.E., & Hommeyer, J.S. (2002). Observed and perceived parenting behaviors and psychosocial adjustment in preadolescents with spina bifida. In B. K. Barber (Ed.), Intrusive parenting: How psychological control affects children and adolescents. Washington, DC: American Psychological Association.

Stone, G., Buehler, C., & Barber, B. K.. (2002) Interparental conflict, parental psychological control, and youth problem behaviors. In B. K. Barber (Ed.), Intrusive parenting: How psychological control affects children and adolescents. Washington, DC: American Psychological Association.

> Table 2-2: Overview of Studies Using Constructs Similar to Psychological Control (p. 29-32)
>
> From: Barber, B. K. (Ed.) (2002). Intrusive parenting: How psychological control affects children and adolescents. Washington, DC: American Psychological Association.

Hauser, S.T., Powers, S.I. Noam, G., Jacobson, A., Weiss, B., & Follansbee, D. (1984). Familial contexts of adolescent ego development. Child Development, 55, 195-213.

Crockenberg, S., & Litman, C. (1990). Autonomy as competence in 2-year-olds: Maternal correlates of child defiance, compliance and self-assertion. Developmental Psychology, 26, 961-971.

Allen, J.P., Hauser, S.T., Eickholt, C., Bell, K.L., & O'Connor, T.G. (1994). Autonomy and relatedness in family interactions as predictors of expressions of negative adolescent affect. Journal of Research on Adolescence, 4, 535-552.

Baumrind, D. (1991). The influence of parenting style on adolescent competence and substance use. Journal of Early Adolescence, 11, 56-95.

Campbell, S.B., March, C.L., Pierce, W.W., & Szumowkski, E.K. (1991). Hard-to-manage preschool boys: Family context and the stability of externalizing behavior. Journal of Abnormal Child Psychology, 19, 301-318.

Steinberg, L., & Darling, N.E., (1994). The broader context of social influence in adolescence. In R.K. Silbereisen & E. Todt (Eds.), Adolescence in context: The interplay of family, school, peers, and work adjustment. New York: Springer Verlag.

Kurdek, L.A., & Fine, M.A., (1993). The relation between family structure and young adolescents' appraisals of family climate and parenting behavior. Journal of Family Issues, 14, 279-290.

Steinberg, L., & Darling, N.E., (1994). The broader context of social influence in adolescence In R.K. Silbereisen & E. Todt (Eds.) Adolescence in context: The interplay of family, school, peers, and work adjustment. New York: Springer Verlag.

Nielsen, D.M., & Metha, A. (1994). Parental behavior and adolescent self-esteem in clinical and non-clinical samples. Adolescence, 29, 525-542.

Kurdek, L.A., Fine, M.A., & Sinclair, R.J. (1995). School adjustment in sixth graders: Parenting transitions, family climate, and peer norm effects. Child Development, 66, 430-445.

Barber, B.K., & Buehler, C. (1996). Family cohesion and enmeshment: Different constructs, different effects. Journal of Marriage and the Family, 58, 433-441.

Mason, C.A., Cauce, A.M., Gonzales, N., & Hiraga, Y. (1996). Neither too sweet nor too sour: Problem peers, maternal control, and problem behaviors in African American adolescents. Child Development, 67, 2215-2130.

Yau, J., & Smetana, J.G. (1996). Adolescent-parent conflict among Chinese adolescents in Hong Kong. Child Development, 67, 1262-1275.

Best, K.M., Hauser, S.T., & Allen, J.P. (1997). Predicting young adult competencies: Adolescent era parent and individual influences. Journal of Adolescent Research, 12, 90-112.

Dobkin, P.L., Tremblay, R.E., & Sacchitelle, C. (1997). Predicting boys' early-onset substance abuse from father's alcoholism, son's disruptiveness, and mother's parenting behavior. Journal of Consulting and Clinical Psychology, 65, 86-92.

Eccles, J.S., Early, D., Frasier, K., Belansky, E., & McCarthy, K. (1997). The relation of connection, regulation, and support for autonomy to adolescents' functioning. Journal of Adolescent Research, 12, 263-286.

Gondoli, D.M., & Silverberg, S.B. (1997). Maternal emotional distress and diminished responsiveness: the mediating role of parenting efficacy and parental perspective taking Developmental Psychology, 33, 861-868.

Herman, M.R., Dornbusch, S.M., Herron, M.C., & Herting, J.R. (1997). The influence of family regulation, connection, and psychological autonomy on six measures of adolescent functioning. Journal of Adolescent Research, 12, 34-67.

Gray, M.R., & Steinberg, L. (1999). Unpacking authoritative parenting: Reassessing a multidimensional construct. Journal of Marriage and Family Therapy.

Appendix 2: Treatment-Focused Assessment Protocol

Treatment-Focused Assessment Protocol

Diagnostic Indicators of AB-PA

Every form of child pathology will evidence a specific and distinctive pattern of symptoms. The trans-generational transmission of *pathological mourning* (Bowlby) from the allied narcissistic (or borderline) personality parent (Beck, Kernberg, Millon) in a cross-generational coalition with the child against the other parent (Haley; Minuchin) is no exception. The pathogenic parenting of an allied parent that creates the child's rejection of a normal-range and affectionally available parent following divorce will be reflected in a set of three definitive diagnostic indica*tors* in the child's symptom display (Childress, 2015)[26]:

1.) Attachment System Suppression. The child will evidence a suppression of normal-range attachment bonding motivations toward a normal-range and affectionally available parent. This child symptom identifies the family pathology as an attachment-related form of pathology.

2.) Personality Disorder Symptoms: The child's symptom display will evidence a set of five a-priori predicted narcissistic personality traits directed toward the targeted parent. These narcissistic personality features in the child's symptom display represent the "psychological fingerprint" evidence of the psychological control of the child by a narcissistic/(borderline) parent. The *primary case* for these narcissistic personality traits is the allied parent who is transferring these deviant attitudes and beliefs to the child through this parent's psychological influence and psychological control of the child. In some cases, the child might evidence extreme anxiety in response to the targeted-rejected parent that will meet DSM-5 diagnostic criteria for a Specific Phobia, but of a bizarre and unrealistic "father type" or "mother type."

3.) Encapsulated Persecutory Delusion. The child symptoms will evidence a fixed-and-false belief that is maintained despite contrary evidence (i.e., a delusion) regarding the child's supposed "victimization" by the normal-range parenting of the targeted parent. This symptom evidenced by the child represents an encapsulated persecutory delusion. As with the narcissistic symptoms, the *primary case* for this encapsulated persecutory delusion is the allied narcissistic/(borderline) personality parent, and the origins of this fixed and false belief is in the "internal working models" (schemas) of this parent's childhood attachment trauma.

A treatment-focused clinical assessment of the pathogenic parenting associated with the trans-generational transmission of disordered mourning should assess for and document the presence or absence of these three diagnostic features in the child's symptom display. The **Diagnostic Checklist for Pathogenic Parenting** (Appendix 4) represents a structured method for documenting the presence or absence of these three diagnostic symptom indicators in the child's symptom display.

Parenting Practices Assessment

In addition to documenting the child's symptom features, the normal-range or problematic parenting of the targeted-rejected parent should also be assessed and documented. The **Parenting Practices Rating Scale** (Appendix 5) is designed to document the results of the clinical assessment regarding the parenting practices of the targeted-rejected parent. Normal-range parenting on the *Parenting Practices Rating Scale* would be parenting at Levels 3 and 4 along with a rating on the "Permissive to Authoritarian Dimension" within the range from 25 to 75. These ratings of parenting practices are based on the clinical judgement of the assessing mental health professional and are a means to document this professional clinical judgement.

---

[26] Childress, C.A. (2015). An attachment-based model of parental alienation: Foundations. Claremont, CA: Oaksong Press.

Treatment-Focused Assessment Protocol: Session Structure

The clinical assessment process is conducted across a set of six to eight targeted clinical assessment sessions.

- **Initial Sessions:** The initial two treatment-focused clinical assessment sessions are to collect history and symptom information from each parent individually.
- **Direct Assessment:** The middle two sessions are a direct assessment of the child's symptoms, either in individual clinical interviews with the child or in parent-child dyadic sessions with the child and targeted parent (at least one dyadic session should be conducted). Clinical probes of the child's symptom features during these sessions can help illuminate the child's symptom display.
- **Parent Response:** The final two sessions are feedback sessions provided to each of the parents to assess the "schemas" of each parent in response to the clinical findings from the prior sessions.

Additional sessions can be added if needed, but typically six to eight sessions should be sufficient to document the presence or absence of the diagnostic indicators of pathogenic parenting associated with the attachment-related pathology of disordered mourning.

Treatment-Focused Report Format

Treatment-focused assessments will produce a targeted report for the Court regarding the treatment requirements needed to resolve the family pathology. Two examples of the type of report available from a treatment-focused assessment protocol, one for a confirmed diagnosis of pathogenic parenting and one for a sub-threshold display of child symptoms, are contained in Appendix 3.

In reports to the Court, it is recommended that the *Diagnostic Checklist for Pathogenic Parenting* and the *Parenting Practices Rating Scale* be included as Appendices to the report for review by the Court in its decision-making function.

Summary of Treatment-Focused Assessment Structure

The treatment-focused clinical assessment uses the following protocol:

1.) **Focus of Assessment:** To assess for the attachment-related pathology of disordered mourning (Bowlby) involving an allied narcissistic/(borderline) parent (Beck; Kernberg; Millon) who is in a cross-generational coalition with the child against the other parent (Minuchin; Haley).

2.) **Diagnostic Checklist for Pathogenic Parenting:** To document the child's symptom features of clinical concern relative to the potential of *pathogenic parenting*.

3.) **Parenting Practices Rating Scale:** To document the normal-range parenting of the targeted-rejected parent or document areas of problematic parenting concern to be addressed in the treatment plan.

4.) **Assessment Session Structure:** A set of six to eight clinical assessment sessions are recommended to document the presence or absence of the diagnostic indicators of pathogenic parenting by an allied narcissistic/(borderline) parent.

Appendix 3: Sample Treatment-Focused Assessment Reports

A Treatment-Focused Assessment Report Example for a Confirmed Diagnosis of Pathogenic Parenting

Date: <Date of Assessment>
Psychologist: <Psychologist's Name>

Scope of Report

A Treatment-Focused Assessment was requested by the Court for the parent-child relationship of John Doe (DOB: 1/15/08) with his mother regarding their estranged and conflictual relationship. This treatment-focused assessment report is based on the following family interviews:

<date>: Clinical interview with mother
<date>: Clinical interview with father
<date>: Clinical interview with child
<date>: Clinical relationship assessment with mother and child
<date>: Clinical interview with mother
<date>: Clinical relationship assessment with mother and child
<date>: Clinical interview with father

Rating Scales Completed (appended)

Parenting Practices Rating Scale (mother)

Diagnostic Checklist for Pathogenic Parenting

Results of Assessment

Based on the clinical assessments, the child displays the three symptom indicators of pathogenic parenting associated with an attachment-based model of "parental alienation" (AB-PA; Childress, 2015):

1) **Attachment System Suppression:** A targeted and selective suppression of the child's attachment bonding motivations relative to his mother in the absence of sufficiently distorted parenting practices from the mother that would account for the suppression of the child's attachment system;

2) **Personality Disorder Traits:** A set of five specific narcissistic/borderline personality disorder features are present in the child's symptom display;

3) **Encapsulated Delusional Belief System:** The child evidences an intransigently held fixed and false belief that is maintained despite contrary evidence (i.e., an encapsulated delusion) regarding the child's supposed "victimization" by the normal-range parenting of the mother (i.e., an encapsulated persecutory delusion).

The presence of this specific symptom pattern in a child's symptom display is consistent with an attachment-based framework for conceptualizing "parental alienation" processes within the family that involve an induced suppression of the child's attachment bonding motivations toward a normal-range and affectionally available parent (i.e., the targeted parent) as a result of the distorted parenting practices of a personality disordered parent (i.e., narcissistic/borderline features, which accounts for the presence of these features in the child's symptom display).

The mother's parenting practices on the *Parenting Practices Rating Scale* are assessed to be broadly normal-range. The mother's parenting would be classified as Level 4, Positive Parenting; Affectionate Involvement – Structured Spectrum. The mother establishes clearly defined rules and expectations for child behavior that are well within normal-range parenting, and the mother's delivery of consequences is fair and is based on these established rules and expectations for child behavior. The mother offers parental encouragement and affection, but these offers of parental affection are typically rejected by the child. The mother's rating on the Permissive to Authoritarian Dimension would be 60, which is well within normal-range parenting. She tends toward the use of clearly established rules and appropriate parental discipline for child non-compliance. The mother's capacity for authentic empathy is normal-range. She is able to self-reflect on her actions and also de-center from her own perspective to adopt the frame of reference of other people. She is not overly self-involved nor does she project her own emotional needs into and onto the child. There are no issues of clinical concern regarding the mother's parenting.

DSM-5 Diagnosis

The combined presence in the child's symptom display of significant attachment-related developmental pathology (diagnostic indicator 1), narcissistic personality disorder pathology (diagnostic indicator 2), and delusional-psychiatric pathology (diagnostic indicator 3) represents definitive diagnostic evidence of pathogenic parenting by an allied parent with prominent narcissistic and/or borderline personality traits, since no other pathology will account for this specific symptom pattern other than pathogenic parenting by an allied narcissistic/borderline personality parent. This set of severe child symptoms warrants the following DSM-5 diagnosis for the child:

    309.4 Adjustment Disorder with mixed disturbance of emotions and conduct

    V61.20 Parent-Child Relational Problem

    V61.29 Child Affected by Parental Relationship Distress

    V995.51 Child Psychological Abuse, Confirmed (pathogenic parenting)

Treatment Indications

A confirmed DSM-5 diagnosis of Child Psychological Abuse warrants the following child protection and treatment response:

1.) **Protective Separation Period:** A period of protective separation of the child from the psychologically abusive parenting practices of the allied parent is required in order to protect the child from ongoing exposure to psychologically abusive parenting practices and allow for the treatment and recovery of the child's normal-range and healthy development. Attempting therapy without first establishing a period of protective separation from the pathogenic parenting practices of the father will continue the child's ongoing exposure to the psychologically abusive parenting of the father that is creating significant developmental pathology, personality disorder pathology, and delusional-psychiatric pathology in the child, and will lead to the child becoming a "psychological battleground" between the treatment goals of restoring the child's healthy and normal-range development and the continuing pathogenic goals of the father to create and maintain the child's pathology.

2.) **Treatment:** Appropriate parent-child psychotherapy should be initiated to recover and heal the damaged parent-child affectional bond with the mother and resolve the impact of the prior psychological abuse inflicted on the child by the father's distorted and psychologically abusive parenting practices in order to restore the child's healthy emotional and psychological development.

3.) **Collateral Therapy:** The father should be required to obtain collateral individual therapy with the treatment goal of fostering insight into the cause of the prior abusive parenting practices.

4.) **End of Protective Separation:** The protective separation period should be ended once the child's symptoms associated with the prior psychologically abusive parenting practices of the father are successfully resolved and the child's recovery is stabilized.

5.) **Restoration of the Relationship with the Abusive Parent:** The restoration of the child's relationship with the formerly abusive parent should include sufficient safeguards to ensure that the psychological abuse of the child does not resume once contact with the father is restored. The demonstrated cooperation of the father with his individual collateral therapy and his demonstrated insight into the cause of the prior psychological abuse of the child would represent important considerations in the level of safeguards needed to ensure the child's protection.

6.) **Relapse:** If the child's symptoms reoccur once the child's contact with the father is restored, then another period of protective separation will be needed in order to again recover the child's normal-range and healthy development, and additional protective safeguards will be warranted prior to once again exposing the child to the pathogenic parenting practices of the father.

Child Response to a Protective Separation

The child may initially respond to a protective separation from the currently allied parent (i.e., the father) with increased protest behavior and defiance. This child response represents an emotional-behavioral tantrum reflecting the child's currently over-empowered status relative to accepting authority (i.e. both parental authority and the authority of the Court). Responding to emotional displays of child tantrum behaviors with calm and steady purpose that restores the child to an appropriate social and family hierarchy of cooperation with Court and parental authority will be important to supporting successful family therapy and the resolution of the child's symptoms. Any concern regarding the child's expressed distress at the protective separation from the currently allied parent (i.e., the father) should recognize that the child is fully capable of ending the protective separation period by becoming non-symptomatic. If the child wishes a termination of the protective separation period, then the child simply needs to evidence normal-range affectional child behavior in response to the normal-range parenting practices of the mother, which is under the treatment-related monitoring of the family therapist.

Ending the Protective Separation Period

The protective separation period from the pathogenic and psychologically abusive parenting practices of the allied parent should be ended upon the successful treatment and resolution of the child's symptoms and restoration of the child's healthy and normal-range development. The treating family therapist should seek Court approval to end the child's protective separation from the pathogenic parenting practices of the currently allied parent (i.e., the father) based on the treatment-related gains achieved. Progress reports to the parents and to the Court from the treating family therapist should be provided at least every six months.

Sincerely,

<psychologist signature>
Psychologist, <license number>

A Treatment-Focused Assessment Report Example for
Sub-Threshold Symptoms for the Diagnosis of Pathogenic Parenting

Date: <Date>
Psychologist: <Psychologist's Name>

Scope of Report

A treatment-focused assessment was requested by the Court for the parent-child relationship of John Doe (DOB: 1/15/08) with his mother regarding their estranged and conflictual relationship. This treatment-focused assessment report is based on the following family interviews:

<date>: Clinical interview with mother
<date>: Clinical interview with father
<date>: Clinical interview with child
<date>: Clinical relationship assessment with mother and child
<date>: Clinical interview with mother
<date>: Clinical relationship assessment with mother and child
<date>: Clinical interview with father

Rating Scales Completed (appended)

Parenting Practices Rating Scale (mother)

Diagnostic Checklist for Pathogenic Parenting

Results of Assessment

Based on the clinical assessments, the child does not display the three symptom indicators of pathogenic parenting associated with an attachment-based model of "parental alienation" (AB-PA; Childress, 2015):

1) **Attachment System Suppression:** A targeted and selective suppression of the child's attachment bonding motivations relative to his mother in the absence of sufficiently distorted parenting practices from the mother that would account for the suppression of the child's attachment system;

2) **Personality Disorder Traits:** A set of five specific narcissistic/borderline personality disorder features are present in the child's symptom display;

3) **Encapsulated Delusional Belief System:** The child evidences an intransigently held fixed and false belief that is maintained despite contrary evidence (i.e., an encapsulated delusion) regarding the child's supposed "victimization" by the normal-range parenting of the mother (i.e., an encapsulated persecutory delusion).

The child's symptom presentation does not fully evidence an intransigently held fixed-and-false belief in the child's supposed "victimization" because the mother's parenting practices are sufficiently problematic to warrant concerns that the child's perceptions of his mother have some component of accuracy. In addition, John expressed an openness to restoring a relationship with his mother if his potentially reality-based concerns can be adequately addressed.

However, John also evidenced a prominent suppression of normal-range attachment bonding motivation toward his mother and he displayed prominent signs of narcissistic personality disorder features in his attitude and responses to his mother. The symptom features in the family also evidenced several Associated Clinical Signs (see attached *Diagnostic Checklist for Pathogenic Parenting*), so that concerns regarding the potential pathogenic influence of the currently allied and supposedly "favored" parent (i.e., the father) continue.

Mother's Parenting Practices

The mother's parenting practices are assessed to be in the Level 3 domain on the *Parenting Practices Rating Scale* (Problematic Parenting), reflecting potentially harsh discipline (Item 12) and high-anger parenting (Item 13). These parenting practices, however, may also be a product of the child's provoking these parenting responses through a high level of child non-compliance and disrespect for parental authority. A Response-to-Intervention (RTI) assessment would help clarify the causal direction for the parent-child conflict.

The child is also likely impacted by chronic exposure to high levels of inter-spousal conflict involving intermittent explosive anger from one spouse directed toward the other spouse (Item 16). While this inter-spousal anger is not directed toward the child, the extent of the high inter-spousal conflict likely creates considerable stress for the child and represents a degree of parental insensitivity for the child's emotional and psychological needs by at least one, and possibly both, parents. Restricting the expression of inter-spousal anger and developing cooperative co-parenting spousal skills of respecting boundaries and for mutual displays of kindness in respectful communication would be in the emotional and psychological best interests of the child.

The mother appears to employ a more disciplinarian approach to parenting involving structured rules and consequences, and her rating on the Permissive to Authoritarian Dimension would be in the 60 to 70 range, which is in the normal-range of parenting. A reduction in parent-child conflict might be achieved by helping the mother expand her parenting options by using increased dialogue and negotiation skills that would shift her rating on the Permissive to Authoritarian Dimension into the mid-range of 45 to 55. However, it should also be noted that the mother's current parenting practices are well within the normal-range for parenting generally, and considerable latitude should be granted to parents to establish rules and values within their families that are consistent with their cultural and personal value systems.

The mother's capacity for authentic empathy with the child appears to be in the normal range. She is able to self-reflect on her own behavior and she is also able to de-center from her own perspective to view situations from alternate points of view. The mother does not appear to become overly self-involved in needing to have her perspective validated, nor does she appear to project her own needs onto the child.

There are no areas of clinical concern related to the mother's parenting.

Treatment Indications

Based on the set of symptom features in child's symptom display and the assessment of the mother's current parenting practices, a Response-to-Intervention (RTI) treatment approach is recommended for a 6-month period to further assess the role of the mother's parenting practices relative to the potential role of pathogenic parental influence from the father in creating and supporting the child's symptomatic relationship with his mother.

1.) Response to Intervention (RTI) Assessment

A 6-month period of family therapy is recommended that includes both mother-child therapy sessions to improve communication and conflict resolution skills as well as collateral sessions with the mother to expand and improve her parenting responses to John.

Authentic Parent-Child Conflict-Resolution: If the mother displays normal-range and appropriate parenting in response to treatment directives, then John's behavior toward his mother should show corresponding improvement (i.e., demonstrating that the child's behavior is under the "stimulus control" of the parent's behavior, meaning that the parent-child conflict is authentic to their relationship features). Changes to the mother's parenting practices will then lead to a resolution of the parent-child conflict.

Authentic Parent-Child Conflict–No Resolution: If the mother is unable to sufficiently alter her potentially harsh discipline and high-anger parenting behavior in response to treatment directives, then this would represent suggestive clinical evidence that the source of the mother-son conflict is potentially authentic to their relationship dynamics, and family therapy should continue to seek changes in the mother's parenting responses toward a more nurturing and affectionate parenting approach to help resolve the parent-child conflict.

Inauthentic Parent-Child Conflict: If, however, the mother displays normal-range and appropriate parenting in response to treatment directives, and John's symptoms continue despite changes in the mother's parenting practices, then this would represent confirming diagnostic evidence that John's behavior is not under the "stimulus control" of his mother's behavior and her responses to him, meaning that he is not responding to authentic difficulties in the mother-son relationship. The continuance of John's symptomatic behavior toward his mother despite changes in the mother's parenting practices would represent diagnostic evidence that John's symptomatic responses to his mother are likely being created by the pathogenic parenting practices of the father (through the formation of a cross-generational coalition of the child with his father against the mother). A treatment plan to address the pathogenic parenting of the father in creating the child's ongoing conflict with the mother should then be developed and implemented (and a period of protective separation from the father's pathogenic parenting may be warranted).

2.) Compliance with Court Orders for Custody and Visitation

All parties, including the child, should comply fully with all Court orders including those for custody and visitation. Failure by the currently allied and supposedly "favored" parent (i.e., the father) to comply with Court orders for custody and visitation should be viewed as non-compliance with treatment, and a follow-up treatment-focused assessment should be initiated (at the written recommendation of the treating family therapist) to determine whether a protective separation of the child from the potentially pathogenic parenting practices of the father is needed to allow for effective treatment.

Child noncompliance with Court orders for custody and visitation, such as refusing custody time-share visitations with the mother, should be ascribed as a serious failure in parenting by the currently allied and supposedly "favored" parent (i.e., the father) representing a parental failure to demonstrate appropriate parental responsibility.

- If the father is instructing the child to comply with the father's directive to cooperate with the mother's custody and visitation time and the child is refusing to comply with the father's directive, then the child is evidencing oppositional non-compliant behavior relative to the father's parental authority and the authority of the Court.

- As the allied and supposedly "favored" parent, the child's behavior is a reflection of the parenting received from the father, so that the child's oppositional non-compliance with the father's parental authority and the authority of the Court is a direct reflection on the father's parenting and his capacity for providing appropriate parental guidance to the child.

A failure to exercise effective parental responsibility and guidance by the allied and supposedly "favored" parent should be viewed as representing the father's non-compliance with the requirements of treatment by failing to exercise appropriate parental responsibility and child guidance as the "favored" and allied parent. The child's refusal to comply with Court orders, including all orders for custody and visitation, and the child's direct defiance of the father's parental authority should trigger a follow-up treatment-focused assessment (at the written recommendation of the treating family therapist) to determine whether a change in the responsible parent is needed to allow for effective treatment and the recovery of the child's normal-range and healthy development.

In any follow-up treatment-focused assessment, primary consideration should be afforded to the treatment needs of the child in establishing the treatment-related conditions necessary for effective treatment. The treatment-related needs of the child should be given precedence over parental considerations of being "favored" or "unfavored" by the child. If the allied and supposedly "favored" parent cannot establish the conditions necessary for the effective resolution of the child's symptoms, then a change in the responsible parent may be necessary due to the then demonstrated parental failure of the allied and supposedly "favored" parent to enact the appropriate parental authority and guidance necessary for the child's successful treatment.

Progress reports to the parents and to the Court from the treating family therapist should be provided at least every six months.

Sincerely,

<psychologist signature>
Psychologist, <license number>

Appendix 4: Diagnostic Checklist for Pathogenic Parenting

Diagnostic Checklist for Pathogenic Parenting: Extended Version
C.A. Childress, Psy.D. (2015/2017)

All three of the diagnostic indicators must be present (either 2a OR 2b) for a clinical diagnosis of attachment-based "parental alienation." Sub-threshold clinical presentations can be further evaluated using a "Response to Intervention" trial.

1. Attachment System Suppression

Present ☐ Sub-Threshold ☐ Absent ☐

The child's symptoms evidence a selective and targeted suppression of the normal-range functioning of the child's attachment bonding motivations toward one parent, the targeted-rejected parent, in which the child seeks to entirely terminate a relationship with this parent (i.e., a child-initiated cutoff in the child's relationship with a normal-range and affectionally available parent).

Secondary Criterion: **Normal-Range Parenting:**

yes ☐ no ☐

The parenting practices of the targeted-rejected parent are assessed to be broadly normal-range, with due consideration given to the wide spectrum of acceptable parenting that is typically displayed in normal-range families.

Normal-range parenting includes the legitimate exercise of parental prerogatives in establishing desired family values through parental expectations for desired child behavior and normal-range discipline practices.

2(a). Personality Disorder Traits

Present ☐ Sub-Threshold ☐ Absent ☐

The child's symptoms evidence all five of the following narcissistic/(borderline) personality disorder features displayed toward the targeted-rejected parent.

Sub-Criterion Met
yes no

☐ ☐ **Grandiosity:** The child displays a grandiose perception of occupying an inappropriately elevated status in the family hierarchy that is above the targeted-rejected parent from which the child feels empowered to sit in judgment of the targeted-rejected parent as both a parent and as a person.

☐ ☐ **Absence of Empathy:** The child displays a complete absence of empathy for the emotional pain being inflicted on the targeted-rejected parent by the child's hostility and rejection of this parent.

☐ ☐ **Entitlement:** The child displays an over-empowered sense of entitlement in which the child expects that his or her desires will be met by the targeted-rejected parent to the child's satisfaction, and if the rejected parent fails to meet the child's entitled expectations to the child's satisfaction then the child feels entitled to enact a retaliatory punishment on the rejected parent for the child's judgment of parental failures

☐ ☐ **Haughty and Arrogant Attitude:** The child displays an attitude of haughty arrogance and contemptuous disdain for the targeted-rejected parent.

☐ ☐ **Splitting:** The child evidences polarized extremes of attitude toward the parents, in which the supposedly "favored" parent is idealized as the all-good and nurturing parent while the rejected parent is entirely devalued as the all-bad and entirely inadequate parent.

2(b). Phobic Anxiety Toward a Parent

Present	Sub-Threshold	Absent
☐	☐	☐

The child's symptoms evidence an extreme and excessive anxiety toward the targeted-rejected parent that meets the following DSM-5 diagnostic criteria for a specific phobia:

Criterion Met
yes   no

☐   ☐   **Persistent Unwarranted Fear:** The child displays a persistent and unwarranted fear of the targeted-rejected parent that is cued either by the presence of the targeted parent or in anticipation of being in the presence of the targeted parent

☐   ☐   **Severe Anxiety Response:** The presence of the targeted-rejected parent almost invariably provokes an anxiety response which can reach the levels of a situationally provoked panic attack.

☐   ☐   **Avoidance of Parent:** The child seeks to avoid exposure to the targeted parent due to the situationally provoked anxiety or else endures the presence of the targeted parent with great distress.

3. Fixed False Belief

Present	Sub-Threshold	Absent
☐	☐	☐

The child's symptoms display an intransigently held, fixed and false belief maintained despite contrary evidence (a delusion) regarding the child's supposed "victimization" by the normal-range parenting of the targeted-rejected parent (an encapsulated persecutory delusion). The child's beliefs carry the implication that the normal-range parenting of the targeted-rejected parent are somehow "abusive" toward the child. The parenting practices of the targeted-rejected parent are assessed to be broadly normal-range.

DSM-5 Diagnosis

If the three diagnostic indicators of attachment-based "parental alienation" are present in the child's symptom display (either 2a or 2b), the appropriate DSM-5 diagnosis is:

DSM-5 Diagnosis

309.4 Adjustment Disorder with mixed disturbance of emotions and conduct

V61.20 Parent-Child Relational Problem

V61.29 Child Affected by Parental Relationship Distress

V995.51 Child Psychological Abuse, Confirmed (pathogenic parenting)

Checklist of Associated Clinical Signs (ACS)

evident	not evident	
☐	☐	ACS 1: Use of the Word "Forced"
☐	☐	ACS 2: Enhancing Child Empowerment to Reject the Other Parent

evident	not evident	
☐	☐	"Child should decide on visitation"
☐	☐	"Listen to the child"
☐	☐	Advocating for child testimony

evident	not evident	
☐	☐	ACS 3: The Exclusion Demand
☐	☐	ACS 4: Parental Replacement
☐	☐	ACS 5: The Unforgivable Event
☐	☐	ACS 6: Liar – Fake
☐	☐	ACS 7: Themes for Rejection

evident	not evident	
☐	☐	Too Controlling
☐	☐	Anger management
☐	☐	Targeted parent doesn't take responsibility/apologize
☐	☐	New romantic relationship neglects the child
☐	☐	Prior neglect of the child by the parent
☐	☐	Vague personhood of the targeted parent
☐	☐	Non-forgivable grudge
☐	☐	Not feeding the child

evident	not evident	
☐	☐	ACS 8: Unwarranted Use of the Word "Abuse"
☐	☐	ACS 9: Excessive Texting, Phone Calls, and Emails
☐	☐	ACS 10: Role-Reversal Use of the Child ("It's not me, it's the child who…")
☐	☐	ACS 11: Targeted Parent "Deserves to be Rejected"
☐	☐	ACS 12: Allied Parent Disregards Court Orders and Court Authority

evident	not evident	
☐	☐	Child disregard of court orders for custody
☐	☐	Child runaway behavior from the targeted parent

Appendix 5: Parenting Practices Rating Scale

Parenting Practices Rating Scale
C.A Childress, Psy.D. (2016)

Name of Parent: _____ Date: _____

Name of Rater: _____

Indicate all that apply.

Child Abuse Ratings: Do <u>not</u> indicate child abuse is present unless allegations have been confirmed. In cases of abuse allegations that have neither been confirmed nor disconfirmed, or that are unfounded, use Allegation subheading rating <u>not</u> Category rating.

Level 1: Child Abuse

☐ 1. **Sexual Abuse**

As defined by legal statute.

☐ Allegation: Neither confirmed nor disconfirmed

☐ Allegation: Unfounded

☐ 2. **Physical Abuse**

Hitting the child with a closed fist; striking the child with an open hand or a closed fist around the head or shoulders; striking the child with sufficient force to leave bruises; striking the child with any instrument (weapon) such as kitchen utensils, paddles, straps, belts, or cords.

☐ Allegation: Neither confirmed nor disconfirmed

☐ Allegation: Unfounded

☐ 3. **Emotional Abuse**

Frequent verbal degradation of the child as a person in a hostile and demeaning tone; frequent humiliation of the child.

☐ Allegation: Neither confirmed nor disconfirmed

☐ Allegation: Unfounded

☐ 4. **Psychological Abuse**

Pathogenic parenting that creates significant psychological or developmental pathology in the child in order to meet the emotional and psychological needs of the parent, including a role-reversal use of the child as a regulatory object for the parent's emotional and psychological needs.

☐ Allegation: Neither confirmed nor disconfirmed

☐ Allegation: Unfounded

☐ 5. **Neglect**

Failure to provide for the child's basic needs for food, shelter, safety, and general care.

☐ Allegation: Neither confirmed nor disconfirmed

☐ Allegation: Unfounded

☐ 6. **Domestic Violence Exposure**

Repeated traumatic exposure of the child to one parent's violent physical assaults toward the other parent or to the repeated emotional degradation (emotional abuse) of the other parent.

☐ Allegation: Neither confirmed nor disconfirmed

☐ Allegation: Unfounded

Level 2: Severely Problematic Parenting

☐ 7. **Overly Strict Discipline**
Parental discipline practices that are excessively harsh and over-controlling, such as inflicting severe physical discomfort on the child through the use of stress postures, using shaming techniques, or confining the child in an enclosed area for excessively long periods (room time-outs are not overly strict discipline).

☐ 8. **Overly Hostile Parenting**
Frequent displays (more days than not) of excessive parental anger (a 6 or above on a 10-point subjective scale).

☐ 9. **Overly Disengaged Parenting**
Repeated failure to provide parental supervision and/or age-appropriate limits on the child's behavior and activities; parental major depression or substance abuse problems.

☐ 10. **Overly Involved-Intrusive Parenting**
Enmeshed, over-intrusive, and/or over-anxious parenting that violates the psychological self-integrity of the child; role-reversal use of the child as a regulatory object for the parent's anxiety or narcissistic needs.

☐ 11. **Family Context of High Inter-Spousal Conflict**
Repeated exposure of the child to high inter-spousal conflict that includes excessive displays of inter-spousal anger.

Level 3: Problematic Parenting

☐ 12. **Harsh Discipline**
Excessive use of strict discipline practices in the context of limited displays of parental affection; limited use of parental praise, encouragement, and expressions of appreciation.

☐ 13. **High-Anger Parenting**
Chronic parental irritability and anger and minimal expressions of parental affection.

☐ 14. **Uninvolved Parenting**
Disinterested lack of involvement with the child; emotionally disengaged parenting; parental depression.

☐ 15. **Anxious or Over-Involved Parenting**
Intrusive parenting that does not respect interpersonal boundaries.

☐ 16. **Overwhelmed Parenting**
The parent is overwhelmed by the degree of child emotional-behavioral problems and cannot develop an effective response to the child's emotional-behavioral issues.

☐ 17. **Family Context of Elevated Inter-Spousal Conflict**
Chronic child exposure to moderate-level inter-spousal conflict and anger or intermittent explosive episodes of highly angry inter-spousal conflict (intermittent spousal conflicts involving moderate anger that are successfully resolved are normal-range and are not elevated inter-spousal conflict).

Level 4: Positive Parenting

☐ 18. **Affectionate Involvement – Structured Spectrum**
Parenting includes frequent displays of parental affection and *clearly structured* rules and expectations for the child's behavior. Appropriate discipline follows from clearly defined and appropriate rules.

☐ 19. **Affectionate Involvement – Dialogue Spectrum**
Parenting includes frequent displays of parental affection and *flexibly negotiated* rules and expectations for the child's behavior. Parenting emphasizes dialogue, negotiation, and flexibility.

☐ 20. **Affectionate Involvement – Balanced**
Parenting includes frequent displays of parental affection and parenting effectively balances structured discipline with flexible parent-child dialogue.

Permissive to Authoritarian Dimension Rating: _____

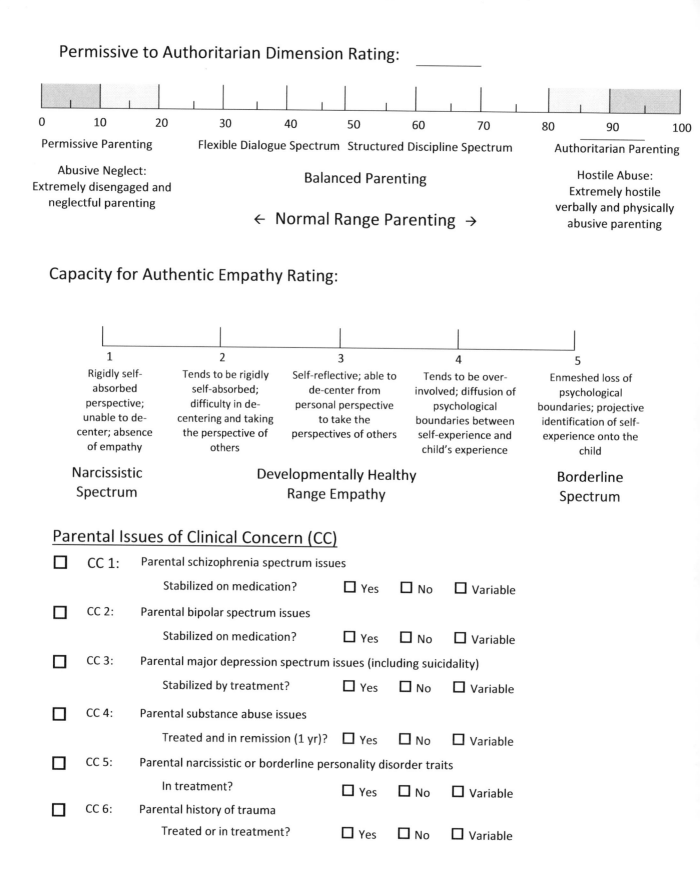

| 0 | 10 | 20 | 30 | 40 | 50 | 60 | 70 | 80 | 90 | 100 |

Permissive Parenting — Flexible Dialogue Spectrum — Structured Discipline Spectrum — Authoritarian Parenting

Abusive Neglect: Extremely disengaged and neglectful parenting

Balanced Parenting

← Normal Range Parenting →

Hostile Abuse: Extremely hostile verbally and physically abusive parenting

Capacity for Authentic Empathy Rating:

1	2	3	4	5
Rigidly self-absorbed perspective; unable to de-center; absence of empathy	Tends to be rigidly self-absorbed; difficulty in de-centering and taking the perspective of others	Self-reflective; able to de-center from personal perspective to take the perspectives of others	Tends to be over-involved; diffusion of psychological boundaries between self-experience and child's experience	Enmeshed loss of psychological boundaries; projective identification of self-experience onto the child

Narcissistic Spectrum — Developmentally Healthy Range Empathy — Borderline Spectrum

Parental Issues of Clinical Concern (CC)

☐ **CC 1:** Parental schizophrenia spectrum issues
　　Stabilized on medication? ☐ Yes ☐ No ☐ Variable

☐ **CC 2:** Parental bipolar spectrum issues
　　Stabilized on medication? ☐ Yes ☐ No ☐ Variable

☐ **CC 3:** Parental major depression spectrum issues (including suicidality)
　　Stabilized by treatment? ☐ Yes ☐ No ☐ Variable

☐ **CC 4:** Parental substance abuse issues
　　Treated and in remission (1 yr)? ☐ Yes ☐ No ☐ Variable

☐ **CC 5:** Parental narcissistic or borderline personality disorder traits
　　In treatment? ☐ Yes ☐ No ☐ Variable

☐ **CC 6:** Parental history of trauma
　　Treated or in treatment? ☐ Yes ☐ No ☐ Variable

Appendix 6: Parent-Child Relationship Rating Scale

Parent-Child Relationship Rating Scale

Childress, C.A. (2015)

Date: _____

Child's Name: _____   Parent's Name: _____

1. Child Attitude: Hostile to Pleasant

```
|----|----|----|----|----|----|----|
1    2    3    4    5    6    7
```

Openly hostile, mean, rude, disrespectful comments

Attitude is generally respectful. No openly hostile, mean, rude, or disrespectful comments. Child accepts displays of affection

Positive, warm, affectionate attitude. Child volunteers displays of affection.

2. Child Cooperation: Behavioral Defiance to Cooperation

```
|----|----|----|----|----|----|----|
1    2    3    4    5    6    7
```

Openly defiant of parental directives.

May complain and argue but is behaviorally compliant with parental directives within 2-3 additional prompts

Cooperative. Minimal to no argument.

3. Child Sociability: Withdrawn to Social

```
|----|----|----|----|----|----|----|
1    2    3    4    5    6    7
```

Withdrawn, sullen, non-communicative. Offers only one-word responses to questions

Is generally responsive to questions, offering elaborated responses. May become withdrawn when upset or angry.

Smiles easily and fairly often. Volunteers self-disclosures of his or her personal experiences.

4. Texting & Phone Call Cooperation

```
|----|----|----|----|----|----|----|
1    2    3    4    5    6    7
```

Frequent arguments and demands to exceed contact limitations

Cooperative and accepting of contact limitations and restrictions

Pleasant and cooperative attitude; understands reasons for contact limitations

5. Parenting Style: Permissive to Structured

```
|----|----|----|----|----|----|----|
1    2    3    4    5    6    7
```

Very lax and permissive. Little to no structure or discipline provided

Blend of behavioral expectations and discipline with negotiation and compromise

Highly structured, rule oriented, expectations for compliance and firm discipline.

Made in the USA
San Bernardino, CA
24 August 2017